THE CURATOR

LISS BREWER

© Liss Brewer 2020

All rights reserved.

Cover Image by Liss Brewer.

Cover created by GermanCreative.

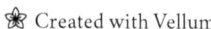 Created with Vellum

CONTENTS

Dedication	v
1. Who Are You Now?	1
The Journals	5
2. Falling	7
The Journals	17
3. Being Pregnant	18
The Journals	25
4. Birth	27
The Journals	33
5. Meeting Her	34
In Memory	37
6. When It's Not Perfect	38
The Journals	41
7. The Worst Day of My Life	42
8. Postpartum	50
9. Chapter Whatever - I'm too tired to remember	61
The Journals	73
10. The Darkness	74
The Journals	83
11. On Being a Teenage Mother	84
The Journals	89
12. Little	90
The Journals	99
13. Siblings	100
The Journals	107
14. What it Means to be a Mother	108
The Recipe Book	115
15. Feeding the Tribe	116
16. Off to School	122
17. On Having It Together	135
18. Tweens	140
The Journals	147

19. The Teenager	148
20. Statistically Unsafe	160
The Journals	167
21. Graduation	168
The Journals	173
22. Leaving Home	174
The Journals	181
23. Omega	183
Acknowledgements	187
About the Author	189

DEDICATION

One time my daughter asked me if I made every part of her, even her heart. When I told her I did, she asked, "And did you make it by taking a part of your heart and putting it inside me?" I had to agree that I had. So, this memoir is dedicated to my children, who all carry pieces of my heart within them.

WHO ARE YOU NOW?

There won't be a day that it happens, you will get no anniversary, but at some point, you will have a moment where you realise your child needs less of you. In the beginning, and indeed for years afterwards, one of the hardest things about being a parent was how much you were needed and how much of yourself you had to put aside for your child. For years I couldn't have a shower uninterrupted. Actually, just the other week I was interrupted by two different children while showering (apple juice requests cannot wait five minutes for Mum to wash herself) but it is far from the norm nowadays. This is a far cry from the days they planted themselves on the bathmat for the entire duration, serenading me with Disney songs. I remember the times I had drawings sent under the door of the toilet so I could critique their artwork while peeing. I recall, while co-sleeping, the shock of being woken from a sound sleep by the heel of a toddler, jutting unexpectedly into my kidney. There were definitely times I feared we would all be sharing the bed when they were 30. And then, slowly over time, I began carrying my sleeping daughter to her own bed. Even at six years old when her limbs were unwieldy and she looked ridiculously large for a 5'2" person to be cradling, I would hold her close to my face so I could kiss the crown of her head before laying her in her bed. At this stage, the bedtime ritual was long and convoluted, two stories or three, just as many songs delivered in my off-key warble. Her insistence that Mama draw on her back until she fell asleep. Over time we dropped a song here and a story there, until one day I was announcing bedtime after only one story and she bounced up to her own room for me to tuck her in to bed. I suppose the 'tucking in' stops at some point too as I don't tuck in my 13-year-old and I can't recall the last time I did, any more than I can recall the last time I carried my youngest, sleeping in my arms, to her own bed.

At some point, much of parenthood becomes 'lasts'. Some of those 'lasts' get lost in the haze and chaos of motherhood – I don't recall the last nappy I changed. Others you get to keep forever, the memory of my eldest daughter walking out of this house, her arms full of boxes, to live in a house of her own. It hits me at intervals, this revelation that our job as a parent is essentially to make ourselves redundant. For, if you do your job well, you will raise children who are not only capable of walking off on their own to successfully manage their own life but barely give you a backwards glance as they go, having no idea that this is a bittersweet moment for you, and only knowing that you are proud of them and excited for their independence.

Who will you be when they're gone?

. . .

For so long I lived in the noise of my children, my true passion, my career, my calling, that sometimes when it's quiet, when they're out of the house, when I have several hours to myself, I realise suddenly that I am still here. In the absence of my children, the silence is deafening. Lulled by the endless school runs and the cycle of the years when change comes slowly, I am shocked to find myself suddenly speeding down the track of 'lasts' as my children one after the other graduate high school, leave home, get jobs, discuss the merits of maternity leave in job contracts for 'down the track'. I watch them take wing and fly while I remain behind, listening to the sounds of my own voice, strange in my ears after years of deferring to the voices of others.

If asked to describe myself any time in the last 21 years the very first word I would have used was 'mother'. I would have used that before 'wife', or 'photographer', or 'editor' or any of the other incarnations of myself I have been in the last two decades. While I will always be a mother, this time of 'lasts', when my children emerge as butterflies, I too go through a metamorphosis of change as I become more of myself. I wander country markets and enquire about pottery lessons. I hook large blankets for no reason except the peaceful monotony of it. I read fat novels and burn candles without fear of small hands knocking them over. I spend hours outside with the plants, keeping careful watch for flowers, new shoots, new life. Sometimes I find caterpillars eating the new growth on the herbs and I carry them to another part of the garden and let them be, giving them the space they need to become butterflies themselves. I have learnt my lessons well. In the quiet solitude of myself I begin to learn who I am.

. . .

I am a woman. A feminist. A good friend in a time of need. An artist. A writer. A lover. A staunch defender of the underdog.

I am the keeper of memories, the curator of my children's childhood, even as I step backwards into the shadows so that they may stand in their own spotlight. The wheel of life turns.

14th April 2019 – The Journals.

I'm not really sure who I am right now. I feel a rising discontent with the way the youth peels from my face and the older me reveals herself underneath. I don't know how to love that me, the one I do not recognise.

I pull at my hair, the dull blandness of it and I wonder if I only spent the money on a good cut and colour, an eye cream, an ionic hairbrush, a...it would change how I feel, that I would wake up feeling like I haven't faded into mediocrity and the years have not taken more than they have given. But I feel like if I did that I would feel silly and strange, like a child, pulling her mother's heels onto her too small feet, tottering along, wearing someone else's truth.

I see no beauty in my body, I turn away from my hands that cradled newborn flesh and kneaded dough, seeing only the lines that creep upon them. These quick fingers, that stitched and sewed. I live in a permanent state of apology, a girl who became a woman that has always been contrite about my own femaleness. And I apologised for the way boys would press themselves upon me as though I lead them there, moving their hands like marionettes. I apologised for love run dry and forgetting the one thing of many as the heaped plate of motherhood overflowed and pieces slipped to the floor. And I apologised for being unable to shoulder the burdens anymore, for the way I broke and bent submissively to my own mind and even as I fought, I apologised for my own shadows that always lived in the corners, snarling and snapping at my heels. I feel the apology rising in my throat, a begging of forgiveness for the way the brass has dulled, the patina of the years that discolour my surface. I want to fight that apology. I want to feel the heat rise in my blood, to drown the apology with a war cry that would rip from my lips!

But the warrior remains silent. Still. Cowed by those years.

Those years.

Those years.
Thoseyearsthoseyearsthoseyears THOSEYEARS! THOSE...
Shh.
I'm sorry.
I apologise.

FALLING

I've been a mother for 21 years. I started younger than most, which meant that on top of the fact I missed my senior formal because having dates that are only 10 months old is frowned upon, it means sometimes if both my daughter and myself are at the liquor store, we both get carded. It does have its perks however, because I can fairly accurately remember what it was like to be a child, I'm not above a fierce game of monopoly and I will absolutely partake in your school yard gossip. My entire adult life I've been someone's mother. I became a woman somewhere between rocking a newborn to sleep and wiping a toddler's face. From 16 to 37, 4 daughters, 2 sons, 3 hospital births, 2 birth centre births, 1 at home. I've breast fed and bottle fed and painstakingly made organic purees, and also watched as my child pushed the dog out the way to eat Science Diet biscuits. This isn't where I ever imagined I would be. But here I am.

It's been harder than I thought it would be to write about my teenage years and finding out I was pregnant. I've always been incredibly candid with my children about my life and the story of finding out I was pregnant at 15. The brief wildness of my youth a cautionary tale that, by turn of luck, had a happy ending. There is still even now, 21 years later, a stigma associated with being a teenage mother. It's like when you hear a story on the news and in the Facebook link there is always a handful of people commenting about how it could have been prevented - as though the people this happened to aren't aware of the chain of events that lead them to where they are in the first place. Any time I mention my daughters age, even now when she is an adult herself, someone will say, "Oh! How old were you when you had her?" I deflect the question with a series of responses I have perfected over decades, unwilling to see the shock in their eyes as they reassess what they think of me and boil me down to that one afternoon in May when I, in the midst of teenage love and a lack of consideration to the consequences, conceived her. How do I marry the fact that teenage pregnancy is an accident carrying life altering consequences with the fact that it brought me one of the best people I know? How do I explain that I'm disappointed in my own actions without devaluing my daughter? How can I illustrate that despite all the incredible hardships of becoming a mother when you're scarcely more than a child, I would do it all over again in a second if it means I get to know her? Being a teenage mother is simultaneously one of the least interesting things about me, and also one of the critical parts of my life that helped shape me into the woman I am today. I am more than the events that made me. I know things should have gone differently and yet, I have no regrets.

I grew up working class in Brisbane in the 80's and 90's. By the time my brothers, 8 and 11 years younger than me were old enough to have a clue, my parents had forged a better position in the world and my brothers received a different kind of life to the one I had. My father was a boilermaker who spent his free time working on his parent's cattle farm and playing golf. He has a love of plants that borders on obsession and throws nothing away that might be useful down the track, even when my mother insists it won't be. With a mop of dark curls, bright blue eyes, and a silly sense of humour he imparted to me, I think he is one of the most resourceful people I've ever met. Long before it was popular and likely from growing up on a property where tank water was a resource not to be wasted, he would diligently bucket the bath water out to his plants in the evening. It took me years to really appreciate my father in the way he deserved. Gone long before I awoke in the morning and home just before dinner, I was alarmed by the way he would fall into long naps on the couch, unable to recognise he was exhausted from the day. My father has an incredible ability to always find something to do. I realise now he is quite left of centre, this is the man my mother and I once found with a large sheet spread over the lounge room floor, with a huge pile of sand and dirt on it, potting his plants in front of the television, casually as you please. It is that eccentricity I now admire that as a teenager I cringed at, when bringing friends home, they would whisper, "Why is your dad watching two televisions at once?" or "Why are there twenty golf balls in the hallway?" or "Why *do* you have so many plants?"

My mother gave me her looks, a keen interest in alternative medicine, and the memory that reading to your child at night is a good way to end the day. She held the job of primary care giver through most of my childhood when she left medical administration when I was 7 to give birth to and care for my 2 brothers, before going back to work in recruitment when my youngest brother went to kinder. My mother was an enigma to me as a teenager, practical, never silly, she didn't indulge in teenage drama, and she could be blunt about her opinions. At the time, I thought she wanted too much from me but I think she was just frustrated by my habit of only giving 80% effort to any given task. Or perhaps, it is just that because she herself is so clever she found it difficult to believe that anyone might not understand something that she herself grasped so easily. Over the years I have come to realise that my mother is quirky in a way that borders on eccentric, and this sits at odds with her practical nature in a way that is both contradictory and beautiful. On any given day, our conversation may be about tax returns and the next about the possibility there is a troll living behind her fridge.

As an only child for the first 8 years of my life I became extremely good at amusing myself, which is one of the reasons I think I would make an excellent hermit. I remember only occasionally being lonely, predominately when my parents moved us interstate when I was 3, where we lived in a caravan beside the beach. This sounds like some kind of idyllic experience but in reality, it meant things like having to go to the public showers every day and eating fish every night, giving me a permanent dislike of the taste. Prior to moving we had lived with my grandparents.

My grandmother is one of the most altruistic people I know. Even when she was gainfully employed she worked raising money for the Sporting Wheelies and later she religiously volunteered with Meals on Wheels for years, only stopping when my grandfather's Alzheimer's progressed to the point where he couldn't be left alone. To this day she still has one of the little tins you put your change into that gets collected for charity. I think she might actually be part angel. The woman *bicycled* to church when pregnant with my mother. I don't even bicycle for pleasure, let alone to worship.

My grandfather though, I loved like the sun and stars. He told me once that he intended to hate me when my mother brought me home from hospital because he was too young to be a grandfather. He also wanted to be *called* Grandfather, like some kind of serious title. Instead he became 'Poppy', and when I came home from hospital I refused to settle in anyone's arms but his. Indeed, my first memory is of him rocking me to sleep when I was an infant. When we moved interstate, he and I clung to each other at the bus stop like spider monkeys, both of us sobbing. Because I missed my grandfather so much I adopted an old man in the caravan park, as even though my grandfather was not yet 50, in my mind he was incredibly old and so this old man would serve as a suitable substitute. I remember lying in a hammock with my mother, walking the beach with my father and the bucket of pipis that sat beside the caravan door. I was warned on many occasions that I wasn't to touch the pipis because it might traumatise them and they would die before my father could use them for bait. I was fascinated by the way they sucked up into their shells however, so occasionally when my parents were both occupied I would quickly give them each a good poke and then stand there panicked, praying for the pipis to come back out before either of my parents came back out and wondered why their 3-year-old was standing guiltily by the bucket.

. . .

After about a year we came back to Brisbane and moved into a house I'm fairly certain would never pass any kind of rental laws now. It was an old Queenslander, run down, with a verandah that slopped slightly towards the side of the house and no glass in the windows. In fact, some of the windows didn't even have fly screens. I don't mean to say the glass was missing, I mean there was never any glass to begin with. This wasn't really the safety issue it seems as anyone wishing to break in would also have to be able to levitate 20 foot off the ground and I don't think anyone was keen to break into a place that looked like the inhabitants couldn't even afford a fly screen. It did make for some issues with mosquitos though and my mother recount one night when I woke up and came into her and my entire face was 'one giant mosquito bite'. Since she was pregnant at the time she insisted that we move house before my brother was born and became exsanguinated by insects.

As such, I mostly grew up in a fairly modern house for the time, a 3-bedroom lowset brick, with walls the previous owners had painted an alarming shade of salmon that I'm sure would be fairly on point according to Pantone's colour of the year for 2019 but was merely offensive in the 90's. There were two high schools within my area, bitter rivals who only became united during inter school sporting events due to their mutual hatred for the high school the next suburb over. I went to the larger of the two, the same high school my parents had attended, a sprawling campus with large old buildings but a more varied curriculum.

As teenagers in the 90's, we were the last generation who didn't carry mobile phones to school and not every house had a computer. The internet was relatively new, the beeping, screeching dial up that may or may not connect... but you certainly had time to go to the loo and make a sandwich before it did. We had the 'homie' phase full of cross colour pants and "Gangsta's Paradise" that morphed into grunge in '96 when we swapped our baggy pants for thrifted shifts and cardigans. We still chose to turn up to a friend's door to see if they were in rather than call the house, probably because the line was engaged due to someone using the dial up. Freshly minted 16-year olds would flaunt school ID's at the corner store to buy a packet of Peter Jackson's for $3.49, slip down to the back oval for a smoke where the evidence could be quickly disposed of before a teacher could make their way down to rouse on us for smoking on school grounds. We wrote bad poetry and formed bands. We listened to Nirvana lyrics like they had been written for us alone. We pierced each other's ears and dyed our hair badly, we wore too much eyeliner and we held within us the keen feeling of immortality that belongs only to teenagers.

In the melting pot of our high school there was me, a halfway girl. Not quite popular and not quite a wallflower. I lived somewhere on the fringe of it all, not fitting in and already wearing too much of my heart on my sleeve. I wasn't smart enough to be an academic, I wasn't sporty enough to be part of the athletic crowd and I didn't smoke enough weed to be one of the stoners. I was a passable student, some C's and B's mostly, but the only subject I really cared about was English. I had written since I was 7, a collection of awful short stories, although my first foray into writing had been thwarted by my mother. I sat down at my grandparent's kitchen table after begging my Nanna for her typewriter and began to compose what I was sure was about to be an incredible novel. I can still remember the basic plot about a woman named Mrs Square whose husband had died in the war. The problem came when I was unsure of the spelling of the word 'fighted' and I went to ask my mother how to spell it.

"Well," she said, "There is no such word. You mean the word 'fought'.

"No, I mean the word 'fighted', like in a war," I patiently explained.

"Yes, that word is 'fought'."

The argument went on in this fashion until in exasperation my mother said, "Look, you can go ahead and write 'fighted' if you want but I'm *not* telling you how to spell it because it's *not* a real word."

I stormed off, ripped my page from the typewriter and pitched it into the bin in a fit of artistic temper that would come back to bite me years later when I became a mother of six children exactly like me in stubbornness.

My 9th and 10th grade English teacher and I butted heads in the same manner during school. Ms Howard was a middle-aged woman with a dark bob who was so tiny even I towered over her. Every time I would come to her with a piece of work I thought was wonderful she would return it full of red pen and a B+. That B+ drove me crazy. I spent two years trying to wear the woman down into an A, putting in more effort, correcting my mistakes and never quite getting there until the day I finally received an A…minus.

When I entered year 11, I thought I had finally gotten out of Ms Howard's shadow but only then did I realise what a treasure it was to have someone constantly pushing you to be better. I could have dealt with the fact I didn't really fit in amongst my peers, or the fact that geography turned out to be so boring I once filled out a report with nonsense that included 'frozen water, otherwise known as ice…" but to lose English to a teacher who flipped through a magazine each lesson while we had 'free writing time' killed the soul of me. I began to miss school more and more, trying to find my place somewhere else. I spent long afternoons at the unit of my friend's boyfriend, a man of questionable employment, who had a habit of stripping stolen cars in his backyard. I took the train into the city and got a job for three days handing out leaflets in the Queen Street Mall for a clothing store wearing black vinyl hot pants and a lime green midriff top. I worked the after-school shift at the corner shop across from the school for the afternoon, deep frying chips and getting paid with a packet of cigarettes and a pluto pup. I spent days on end writing in the park alone, filling page after page of loose leaf paper. It felt like I had all the pieces of my life in front of me and I was trying to get them to fit in any way that made sense. All of this was completely unknown to my mother of course, who had no idea that when I went off to school in the morning I rarely made it there. It was a wayward, driftless few months of my life and I think I was standing at the crossroads where I was either going to fall into complete delinquency or saddle up and go back to school and make a crack of it. But before either of those things could come to pass, I fell pregnant.

30th of April 2007 – The Journals

I wondered whether I should make a little joke at the beginning of this entry. Something about not giving up or whatever. But I really don't want to trivialise the blessing of it, so I won't.

The last couple of days I have been very tired. I sleep in, I go to bed late. I felt a bit ill on and off. My temperature kept climbing. I wanted to get the results of my hormone test, particularly the one that would tell me whether or not I even ovulated this cycle. I ended up having the most frustrating conversation with the receptionist who told me the results were in but the doctor hadn't opened them yet and also the doctor wouldn't be in until tomorrow. I know they seemed like just a little thing but for me they were everything.

We did the grocery shopping and I caved and bought a test but when I went home and was scared to take it. My hands were shaking as I waited for that inevitable negative. After about 10 seconds the second line came up and at first, I thought I was seeing things, but then, oh god! It was so dark! I stood at the door and said to my husband, "I'm pregnant?" And we both went to stand over the test taking it in before we just kind of went our separate ways, I guess dealing with the emotions of it.

Then I suddenly burst into tears, that loud, choking kind and he came barrelling into the room asking what was wrong.

But nothing was wrong.

It was that everything was right.

It was serendipity.

BEING PREGNANT

When I was pregnant with my youngest son I had hyperemesis, I don't think I've ever been so sick in my life. I would crawl into the shower and lie on the floor until the hot water ran out. I had pressure sores on my wrists from sea sickness bands. I lived on Ondansetron, which was expensive and not easy to get. Doctors acted as though I were a drug seeker, looking for a hit while I'm vomiting in a bag in their office, as though anyone would just *want* to pay $120 a week in medicine. I mean, I get it. We do want to reduce the number of pharmaceuticals a pregnant person is putting in their body. But I was planning a homebirth, people. I had a herbalist. I wore hemp clothes and bought organic vegetables. I just wanted to keep down some water and not have my toddler ask me if I was going to die.

Pregnancy seems to be an act of progressively surrendering more of your body to the person growing inside you. Your body, once a benevolent being that assisted you with life and only rarely complained, is now a demanding force wanting a certain food at 3am, sending you to sleep like a fairy tale princess in the early afternoon, and vomiting at the slightest provocation. Pregnancy can be gruelling, the morning sickness, stretch marks, constipation, sore breasts, varicose veins, discomfort whilst sleeping, the fear that if you drink a cup of coffee your child will be born with three heads – all of them asking for a latte. Everyone seems to have an opinion on what you should be doing with your body, which gives you a chance to get used to it so when everyone has an opinion on what you should be doing with your child you're more likely to just flip them off behind their back rather than cry in a corner about all the ways you're failing as a parent. In the midst of all your discomfort and distress you still manage to feel guilty for not enjoying the miracle of life more, a fact some assholes will remind you of - even while you're complaining about having to vomit while cooking dinner for your small children and get back in time to flip the steaks before they burn. Here is the thing... those people suck. You are absolutely allowed to feel miserable and complain and still be grateful you're going to have a child. Parents are complicated creatures and you're about to become a walking contradiction anyway. If you ask any parent how parenthood is going they may answer, "Awful." And if you ask them the next day they may say, "Delightful." and both will be true. The miracle of pregnancy can absolutely sit side by side with the fact you feel positively awful.

In other ways, I didn't mind pregnancy. It was somewhat freeing to be able to rid yourself of the constraints of what society tells you that you should look like and just concentrate on being as healthy as you can be for the growing child within you. Ideally, we would all be body positive all the time but I simply haven't achieved that kind of enlightenment yet. Pregnancy allowed me to accept my body as it was since it was going to look different next week anyway. As such, I relished in the ripe bulge of my stomach, the heaviness of my breasts and my full shiny head of hair.

It is a strange thing, being host to someone else. I think even without the associated hormones it would take some getting used to, but the hormones – designed to support the growing foetus and facilitate birth – truly do pack a punch. It seemed my body progressively got more fed up with being pregnant, until by the end of my last pregnancy I had Symphysis Pubis Dysfunction, Hyperemesis Gravidarum and Gestational Diabetes or SPD, HG and GD , a bit of an alphabet soup which basically made me miserable and ready to sell my soul to the devil to go into labour and get that baby out of my body. Still, at risk of sounding like one of those assholes and acknowledging my own contradictory behaviour, there *is* something a little bit magic about waiting for your child. This growing swell of love that happens even as your stomach obstructs your view of your toes. It's the wait, the anticipation, the hope. More than anything I think it's the hope. The very act of having a child is a rebellion. We all know that the world is a bit of a horrible place at times, the oceans are polluted, the rainforest is being logged, there is war and famine and sometimes idiots in charge who make us all concerned. And yet…within your child, within yourself, is a little bit of light, your hope for a future that is worth living and the wish that your child may be a part of the wonderful fabric of humanity. It is the acknowledgement that even in the darkest of moments, goodness still exists and that it is what will endure. A child is the secret of your own immortality, a person to carry the tales of yourself, your parents, your ancestors into the future so that you may live on when someone cooks a recipe passed down, smiles with your dimples, names their own child after you – even generations down the track. We can deconstruct it and reduce it to science and biology, but I still believe there is something spiritual in having a child. The alchemy of a dream turned flesh.

At 16, I wasn't quite there on the magic spiritual part. Instead it was more like I had exactly 9 months to do a short crash course in parenting and how to be an adult. Prior to this point in my life, the biggest responsibility I had was not letting down my double's partner at the semi-finals for tennis and ensuring the garden was free of rubbish when the teachers made the students do 'Emu Parade'. I'm sure my daughter's father felt the same.

When I first began this memoir, I intended to do it without mentioning my daughter's father at all, partially out of respect from him and partially because this tale was about my journey through motherhood, and if he wanted to tell his story of fatherhood he was welcome to write a memoir of his own. It is impossible to tell it without talking about teenage love however, because without it, my daughter would not exist. I say that because I wasn't really the sort of girl who slept with a bunch of different guys, or even dated a bunch of different guys. I flirted, I wore short skirts in order to attract their attention but, in truth, I mostly only had eyes for one guy. Like me, he existed somewhere in the in-between in high school, but he was charming in a way that seemed to captivate a lot of different girls. He was artistic, he had long fingers and beautiful hands which I can still remember so clearly to this day that if I possessed the talent to sketch I'm sure I could do it from memory alone. He also had a wonderful ability to be silly and not really worry if he might *look* silly doing whatever he was doing to make people laugh. However it may have ended for us, I believe that at the time, I loved him as much as any teenage girl can love a boy. He wasn't the love of my life, but we did love each other – very much. If we hadn't, perhaps our story would have gone in a different direction and my daughter wouldn't be here today, filling the world with her presence. Or maybe it would have gone exactly the same. I only know that for us, the fact that we were in love certainly played a role in deciding that we wanted to keep this baby and that for better or worse, we were going to try our best to raise a child together.

And so, both of us, in our own muddling ways began to prepare for the arrival of our daughter as best we could, with limited resources and not a lot of knowledge. I imagine that had I been a pregnant teenager today I would join a Facebook group and have access to the internet to Google the variety of feelings I was experiencing, both emotionally and physiologically. But as I was a pregnant teenager in 1997, my resources were limited to books and the wisdom of the women I knew who had borne children before me. In some ways, I think that is wonderful because I look back on it with rose coloured glasses and imagine these wise women passing on their experience like passing a dish at a table, allowing me to take what I needed, much as I am doing for you right now. Probably my largest source of information came from my daughter's grandmother, my boyfriend's mother. I spent a lot of time during my pregnancy with her, drinking tea as she told me about her life, her childhood, her own mother, her pregnancies and births. She arranged for me to join a craft class and there I learnt how to sew and quilt and met other women who told me their own stories. I listened to them all and wondered what my journey would be. Every single blessed and cursed thing that could happen to a woman in pregnancy or birth – I heard it. Women would revel in the retelling of their stories, the joy of a long-awaited pregnancy, the shock of grief caused by loss, the morning sickness, the haemorrhoids, the sweat of labour, the stitches, the blood, the pain, the quiet meeting of your child. Even my great-grandmother chimed in and advised me that the sure-fire way to cure my iron deficiency was the way she had done it during her pregnancies – to eat a handful of raw mince, which I politely thanked her for but declined to put into practice.

In a more practical sense, I was also the recipients of many hand-me-down items, baby clothes and furniture, crockery and pans. We carefully shopped each week, learning how to budget. Grocery shopping became a weekly adventure to me, I rarely left the house except to visit relatives and attend my craft class. As my pregnancy had progressed I found I retreated more into myself, withdrawing from old friends whose lives I could no longer relate to, I felt poised on the edge of my new life, waiting. Not once did I look back at where I had been but moved doggedly forward, with a certainty that I now admire. I had no room inside me for anything but the promise of my child. It felt in some way, that I was stripping away layers of myself, discarding the parts of me I no longer needed in my new life, to reveal the shape of the woman I was to become. I think all women transition like this, but for me, moving from child to mother in 9 short months, I felt the change keenly.

. . .

One morning, when I was pregnant with my daughter, I woke to find that overnight my breasts had become covered in a spider webbing of thin, red stretchmarks, reaching out from my nipples like sun rays. I was surprised by the suddenness of their arrival, that my body had changed so much overnight. That was what the entire pregnancy felt like to me. As though I went to sleep a girl in her bed surrounded by stuffed animals and woke up a woman.

24th of June, 2014 – The Journals

When a woman is giving birth, in the beginning the trials of labour are almost comical. You can smile through the contractions, even though they hurt. You laugh. You still make jokes. The pauses between them are longer and you get to rest and recover. But as labour progresses things start to get more intense. The pains are longer, the hurt is deeper. Shortly before the pushing part there is a stage called transition.

In transition women give up. This is the time where the hurt is too much to bear.

"I can't do this."

Sometimes said with anger. Sometimes despair. Sometimes it is delivered matter-of-factly. But always she believes it to be true.

At this time, she must be rallied.

"You CAN do this."

"You ARE doing this."

"You MUST do this."

Because there is no other way. There is nobody but her. And the time is here.

Transition is short in minutes, but the despair, the helplessness and the darkness lasts a long time for a woman. And then, all of a sudden, she will rally. And she will barely remember the shadows.

You can do this. You are doing this. You must do this.

I vividly remember that moment when I had E. I had wanted an epidural and they seemed to take forever getting it ready. And it was all laid out, all these strange bits and pieces on a tray. I had been alternating between showers and the birthing stool and had given up all semblance of modesty. My friend, Char who had come along to photograph the birth is kneeling down in front of me and I'm totally stark naked with a small towel on my lap and I couldn't care less she was seeing far more of me than our friendship had thus far consisted of. And finally, the epidural was ready and the midwife said, "I just need to check you first." I knew this meant she was going to find out

THE JOURNALS

how far along I was because if I was too close to delivering they wouldn't give me the epi, and I could already tell by the depths of the pains that I was about to deliver.

Man, I don't think anyone has ever been so reluctant to get an exam. And as soon as she checked and announced I was almost ready to push I turned and looked at my husband and said, "Can you BELIEVE I'm doing this without an epidural AGAIN?"

There is this photo Char took of me, just before I began to push, where I am blankly staring down the bottom of the bed, my hair is all plastered down and you can just tell I've given up. I remember another contraction picking me up and wringing me out and I lay there in its wake, again and again.

And the midwives would say, "Just push when you feel you need to."

But I never have gotten the urge to push no matter how long I wait. For me, it's always been a conscious choice to begin... and I wasn't ready. I didn't want to. I couldn't. And then another contraction hit and I remember thinking that if I didn't rise up and push then there would be no end. In some ways, during transition, a woman decides to save herself. She becomes her own hero. In the next photo, I am pushing, my face rigid with the effort, but determined. And then she was here. All 6lb 15oz of her. She was perfect.

BIRTH

When you are pregnant you focus heavily on preparing for the birth. Preparing for birth is a bit of a misconception because, while of course you have to prepare for it and do things like pack a hospital bag, you really can't prepare like you would a science exam. The variables are infinite. Every one of my children's births were different; I could no more plan for my sixth child's birth than I could my first. In my experience, you don't actually 'plan' for birth as so much attempt to manage it the same way you might attempt to manage a boulder careening down a hill. Of course, like absolutely everything in parenting there is someone out there who had an easy time of it. Someone who had a lovely birth experience full of scented candles and loving looks between themselves and their partner but for me it's mostly been sweaty, uncomfortable with a good smattering of swearing thrown in for good measure. I don't tell this to my daughters. I tell them that birth is 'hard work' because I read somewhere that the culture of frightening women with birth horror stories makes it hurt more and I thought maybe not contributing to that might make up for 21 years of mediocre dinners. The flip side to this is if no one is baldly honest with you, you can be fooled into thinking it's like a hard work out at the gym (I wouldn't know because I have never had a hard work out in my life but I like to imagine). I distinctly remember after the birth of my first child accusingly asking my mother, "Why didn't you tell me how much it hurt?" and her looking at me in exasperation and responding with, "Well, what did you *think* it was going to feel like?" Which is a fair response, actually.

When I was pregnant with my first I didn't know this was a fly-by-the-seat-of-your-pants situation, so I read books and asked questions and attended the birthing classes at the hospital. I told myself those stories about women having babies out in the fields and then going straight back to work in an effort to tell myself that I would indeed be able to get through this without losing my mind. I had decided to decline all pain relief and have a 'natural birth' – a term I dislike as it implies there is such a thing as an 'unnatural birth', which there is not. The major flaw in my plan was that up until that point the worst pain I had ever felt amounted to a skinned knee while rollerblading, and so it's not that remarkable I was left breathless by the battlefield my body became during childbirth.

When my waters broke in the dark of the night, I could barely even wrap my head around the fact she was going to be born. A baby still felt like a hypothetical. As the first pains gripped me, I smiled and joked, buoyed along by the novelty of this new experience. Hours later they became worse with a suddenness that literally dropped me to my knees, panting on the floor like a dog. They went on and on, the sun rose, the clatter of the breakfast trolley being wheeled around. People came and went;

my boyfriend's mother began to doze beside me before going home to sleep and I have a hazy recollection of my aunty sitting in a chair in the room for a time before leaving me to my work. And through it all, the contractions buffeted me like a small boat on the vast and angry ocean. I screamed. I screamed until my throat was raw, until nurses poked their heads in to look at me with alarm and slight disapproval. I'm sure if anyone had of offered me an epidural at that point I would have taken it. But no one did. So, I just kept asking how much longer as though I were a child on a road trip. After lunch, I began to doze between contractions, exhausted after 10 hours of labour and not sleeping for over 24, my dreams were disjointed and hallucinatory. Mostly, I dreamt of the ocean, the waves rolling in and me on them, riding the wave. This would sound almost beautiful except for the absurdity of the fact that in my dream I was surfing next to Roger Rabbit. I wave at Roger and he waves at me. He motions me over conspiratorially, "Hey," he says, "I'm Roger. *You're* Rabbit."

Another contraction wakes me. I scream.

It's a wonder after the agony of the first birth that I ever went back to have another. But whether it was increased pain tolerance or simply the difference in births, I never again screamed the way I did that first time. To be honest, I think I suffered most from my lack of support during the birth of my first daughter. I would have benefitted from a good coach to tell me to relax my jaw, to count out the seconds, to calm me and bring me out of the cloud of fear and shadows that I was surrounded by. However, with my next babies, I gained confidence in my body and its ability to stretch and yawn and become the doorway to the world for my children. For the most part, I seem to find the first 8cms to be fairly easy work, I huff and pant, roll and rock my hips, keep my body relaxed and surrender to the process. Then it all changes.

The hardest part of childbirth for most women seems to be transition. It's this period of time where your contractions slow or stop for a period as the body prepares for the next stage where you will push your child into life. At this point, you are exhausted, you are shocked at the pain you've endured and you don't believe you have the strength or courage to continue. You may despair. At many points in my life I have felt this way and reminded myself of transition. I would remind myself at 3am as I walked the hall with a sleepless newborn. I would remind myself when I was in the darkness of postnatal depression. I would remind myself when I miscarried. I would remind myself that even when you think all is lost, when you fear that you cannot go on – that women do. In the midst of that despair, the exhaustion, the fear, you reach down inside yourself and you rally. You feel the contractions that until that point had been kicking your ass – and you push back. You rise to the challenge of battle and you grit your teeth and summon your war cry. As you stare into the face of despair, you roar and banish the shadows. I will never get tired of women's stories of that moment and I watch for it when I see photos my friends post of births they have shot for clients. In one photograph, there will be the woman, her head back and eyes closed and her face wearing the lines of effort…the next, the steely grit of a warrior. And then, the joyous lightness of the newborn, whose first cries shatter the darkness. Oh, yes. I know why I went back to babies again and again.

At some point, just before 3pm they wheeled me from the

maternity ward to the delivery suite proper, where I would give birth to my child. I wasn't capable of walking so they pushed me in a wheelchair, and I remember the women in the ward looking up as I went past, laying eyes on the woman whose screams they had been listening to for hours. I was put into a delivery gown and helped up on to the bed. Prior to this I had imagined that during labour I would have a midwife with me all the time, perhaps doing those short puffy breaths they show on television and that someone would say, "good, good" at the end of the contraction. I imagined they would feed me ice chips and in general keep me abreast of any progress I had made. Instead I was left to labour for long stretches, with no guideposts to show me the way, I felt as though I were swimming in an endless darkness.

When I had first arrived at hospital, my boyfriend's mother sitting with me in the waiting room outside of the delivery suite where I would shortly be ushered into so they could confirm that my water had broken, and we listened to the sounds of a woman giving birth. Her screams were the most real thing I had ever heard. Until that point, everything in my life had been relatively sanitised, polite, civilized. This woman bellowed like she was being tortured. I turned to my mother in law, alarmed and she laughed and said, "Just wait." She wasn't being cruel, it was just that in my panic, she had noticed something I hadn't – that the noise had stopped. And then, from the silence a cry rang out, the pure, crystal clear sound of a newborn's first breath, the laugh of joy from the woman who had one moment before been screaming.

My mother in law wrapped her arm around me and squeezed, "See? What did I tell you?"

. . .

Floating in my own pain, I couldn't recall that this would end in laughter, I couldn't recall that it would end at all. Finally, as though they had been summoned by some unheard chime the room began to fill with people. From the depths of my own pain I had a moment to realise how absurd they all looked, most of them standing around doing nothing and watching me as though I were on stage, waiting for me to rise to the occasion and push out my daughter.

I bore down again and again, not sure I was doing it correctly, although a midwife assured me I was making progress. Then suddenly, I felt a hard pressure inside of me, the baby's head at the doorway. I felt hyper aware of every sensation in my body, a surreal feeling that I was experiencing everything under a microscope. It felt like I could hear the blood rushing through my veins, the *shoo, shoo* of a steam train. I felt like I could hear beads of sweat breaking through my pores like bubbles popping. I thought I could literally hear my flesh tear as her head was born, a sound like stitching being ripped. Then, her body, slippery as a fish, sliding out into the hands of the midwife.

1st of July, 2019 – The Journals

My daughter's grandmother said her husband saw their daughter before she was ever born. He was driving along and saw her face appear before him. He said he knew they would have a daughter. My mother in law had given birth to 3 sons by that point and didn't believe it. She was certain she would have another boy. But he remained adamant - he had seen her. And when she delivered, everyone told her she had a daughter, but she couldn't believe it until she saw her with her own eyes. I have never had the gift of seeing my children before they were born but each time I could barely comprehend them as actual beings until they were laid in my arms. It's strange. You carry them for 9 months, you have been closer to them than anyone except maybe your own mother, but until you see them they're not entirely real. Then suddenly, this little weight in your arms is so substantial. Thrust into reality.

MEETING HER

The first time I met my daughter was in the quiet, darkened room of the delivery suite. Not 10 minutes before there had been a collection of nurses, paediatricians and obstetricians, all standing by while I pushed her into the world, shocked by the ferocity of the pain, and sure I was about to split in two. Now, suddenly, they had all departed leaving myself and a single nurse, quietly doing paper work in the corner. The room smelled of blood, disinfectant and something earthy and primal that I couldn't recognise. The clock ticked quietly away.

I had not seen my daughter yet. Born at 36 weeks she had been immediately whisked to a corner of the room to be checked, my only glimpse of her a red blur as she passed between hands. She lay quietly in a crib across the room, a bundle of blankets. I was shaky and exhausted from the birth, alarmed by the blood, unsure of my ability to stand without falling over. I was still a young girl who had spent all of her life under the direction of others, I wasn't sure of the rules now. I hadn't yet learned that to be a mother you must also be a warrior, a defender, an advocate. I didn't yet know that to be a woman you must sometimes shout or you will never be heard. Instead, I very timidly asked the nurse if it was okay if I held my baby. I believe if it had been any one of the other doctors and nurses in the room with me that day, I likely would have been told no. The air of disapproval at my current circumstances during birth had hung thickly in the air. She looked up from her paper work as if surprised to find me still there, she glanced at the door, "She's supposed to go to the special care nursery, she came too early… but…I suppose you can hold her for a few minutes." She walked across the room and picked up the bundle and placed it in my arms. I marvelled at the creature in front of me, scarcely believing she had come from within me. Her hair was black and wavy, crimped like sheep's wool. Her mouth was a tiny rosebud. She moved in my arms and began to make small cries, no louder than a baby bird and this surprised me too, the realness of her, when for so long she had seemed no more substantial than a daydream. I rocked her instinctively, shushing her softly, "Shh. Shh, baby girl."

I think everyone has this moment after their child is born, sometimes moments after, sometimes weeks, when all the hustle of birth is over, when everyone has gone home or left the room and it's just you and your child and you look at them taking in the world around them and they look so wise that you can almost believe they know more about the world than you do. There is a video of my second eldest, taken by her father moments after she was born while I was in the shower and the two of them were alone. The video is black and white and she is a small bundle in a tiny hat, her little hand holding her chin, her fingers wiggling back and forth, her big eyes blinking as she looks around quietly and contentedly. When his mother found the video she said, "I almost felt as though I shouldn't be watching it, it seemed so personal." And I know exactly what she means, as he talks to her quietly, telling her how beautiful she is, that he is her Daddy, and that she looks so much like her big sister who she will meet as soon as Grandma brings her up. That was his moment, the quiet getting to know you that happens when you hold a miracle and see it for what it truly is. Mine happened when I held my eldest daughter, my first little love, and was shaken by the wonder of how my whole world was now in my arms. She snuffled at the stiff fabric of my green hospital gown, her head butting softly against my chest.

For the last few months of pregnancy I had felt like the loneliest person in the world. I didn't know how to prepare for a child, I didn't know how to prepare to become a mother. While my friends had been studying for their year 11 finals, I had been studying baby books. I read everything I could get my hands on. I asked seasoned mothers I knew, decades older than myself, and I stored away the information they gave me like jewels. But nothing at all prepared me for meeting my child because emotions cannot be studied and learned, they must be felt. I stroked her cheek with a feather light touch and I became a mother.

IN MEMORY

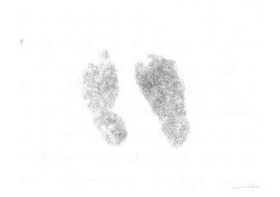

WHEN IT'S NOT PERFECT

Some children come along unexpectedly but, as I say to my two children who were unplanned, they were a surprise but never a mistake. Some children you plan long before you ever see those two lines on a test. Having not dealt with the pain and frustration of infertility myself I won't even attempt to describe it; women far more knowledgeable than I have done a far better job and there are plenty of resources and support both online and in print for women who are struggling to try to conceive. I have, however, had friends and family who waited many years to have a child and some for whom that dream was never realised and I do recommend that anyone who has loved ones travelling that journey tries to be mindful of feelings your joyous news may hold for them. There is no one size fits all guide to empathy unfortunately, so everyone will be different, but I do remember one of my friends telling me that she always appreciated being sent an email or text message with a 'heads up' rather than being told in person or over the phone. She said it allowed her time to feel all her feelings and process them so that she could then respond with love and happiness for her friend or family member. This may be true also for those who have suffered a loss, either miscarriage, stillbirth or the loss of an infant or child. News of a child is always good, your loved ones will be happy for you, but we are also imperfect people and sometimes our own feelings come out.

I have had the misfortune of miscarrying several times and some of them rocked me harder than others. In particular, I remember a pregnancy I lost at 11 weeks after bleeding and cramping for the last 3 weeks and trying as best I could to lie down while trying to parent my small children at the same time. At 11 weeks, the foetus is only the size of a fig, a slip of a being, and yet in my mind I had already thought of names, imagined my life with this child, began thinking of a colour for the nursery. Time and again I went to the hospital thinking I was going to be told it was all over, and every time the heartbeat came back strong and with each visit I dared to hope a little more. When I eventually went in and the ultrasound was still and silent, I was devastated. When I came home I felt fragile, as though my heart and soul had been battered and I was barely held together. I waited for the wounds to heal over, consoling myself that scar tissue was thick and strong but what I discovered was that even when I felt fine, the slightest brush would send my heart to bleeding again. I felt unanchored, like a piece of tin roofing flapping in the breeze. I couldn't watch anything with pregnancy or babies in it and so I spent a week in bed watching reruns of Buffy because I knew there wasn't going to be an unexpected baby on it to hurt me all over again. At the end of that week I thought I had recovered from my grief and then, browsing through Flickr I saw a photo someone had posted of a positive pregnancy test and I felt as though I were winded, literally doubled over holding my stomach and gasping for breath.

We try to minimise the hurts of miscarriage, particularly early miscarriage. I have heard women do it over and over, as though grief can ever be measured. I've heard women recount their loss and then immediately qualify it by saying, "I know I was only XYZ along". No. Grief is your very own thing. It does not need to be measured against anyone else's loss to be valid, painful and real to you. For me sometimes the loss was that raw, horrific sadness I mentioned above and yet there was a time when I felt so full of pure, unadulterated rage that I was sure if I dared unleash even the smallest amount I would split the world in two. My fury felt telekinetic and I was single-handedly keeping the world together by not opening the door to it. It may be either of those things, or it may be despair or apathy or a cocktail of emotions and all of that is okay. There is not a single person on the planet who is allowed to tell you how to grieve. You get to own the feelings from your own 'worst day of your life'.

28th of August 2017 – The Journals

At first it consumes everything. But slowly you grow around it until you find yourself managing the grocery shopping, worrying about something mediocre, you watch a television show, you startle yourself by laughing because for a time you weren't sure you would – ever again. Sometimes it is still big, bowling you over like a wave at the beach but some days, and they become more often, it is like a pebble in your shoe. It's so small. You can walk miles while that pebble of grief rolls around. Always aware, but liveable. Survivable. It becomes a bearable burden.

But. Oh.

The weight of the memories I have to carry for the both of us.

THE WORST DAY OF MY LIFE

My middle daughter is my rainbow baby. A rainbow baby is the child born after the loss of another. They're the child that can never erase the pain of who you lost but remind you there is joy in the world.

The worst day of my life happened in 2001. I didn't know when I woke up that anything would be different. In fact, I was looking forward to the day ahead because I was 15 weeks pregnant and was going for an ultrasound that day. The pregnancy was hard from the start. At 5 weeks I had begun bleeding – sure I had miscarried I already had grieved the loss of that baby. The next day I went for an ultrasound and saw a tiny bean floating unscathed. A repeat ultrasound a few weeks later after the bleeding stopped showed a flickering heartbeat. However, the tech saw a shadow of something and said I should go to the RBWH for a better ultrasound. That was the one I was scared for. But there they waved the wand over my stomach, the gel cold on my skin and declared everything perfect. They told me to book in later for a follow up but everything seemed great, I had nothing to worry about.

By 15 weeks I thought it was just a cool chance to see my baby again. I felt like it was a boy. My stomach had already begun to swell beneath my pants, I had bought the next size up and joked I would need maternity clothes soon. I could feel the faintest of butterfly wings sweeping inside me as he swam in his watery cocoon. I had picked names. I wondered what Christmas would be like this year with a tiny baby. I wondered if my daughters would be excited by their new sibling.

On the worst day of my life I lay in a thin table in a dimly lit room while my husband sat beside me, anxious to see our baby. A woman I had never met squirted gel on my stomach and a smooth wand glided across the small rise of my abdomen. I knew instantly something was wrong. Here was my baby who was waving his arms and legs in a greeting, here was his rounded stomach and tiny face. But, oh, his head. I can never describe the quiet of that room. The silence as she repeatedly went back over his skull and viewed how misshapen it was. From the front on, he was a baby like any other. From the side, his skull stretched upwards, elongated and almost twice the length it should be. I kept wanting to say to her to please go back to the front view. I didn't want to see what I was seeing. And I couldn't pull my eyes away.

"Excuse me," she said, and left the room.

The quiet between myself and my husband hung thickly in the air. What comfort could I possibly offer him at this time when I knew in my heart that something was terribly wrong? My thoughts spun out in a thousand different directions. Our baby is sick. Something is wrong. I thought of all the ways they could fix babies now, even doing in utero surgery. This was terrifying but they would fix him.

The woman came back with a man. I could walk past him in the street and never recognise him. I have no idea what he looked like. But his words are scarred into my memory. He looked a long time. And then he spoke, "What do we have here? Well, what we have here is a bad baby. A very bad baby. This baby is incompatible with life, a nurse will discuss your options."

He left and I excused myself to the detached bathroom leaving the woman and my husband alone in the darkened room.

Incompatible with life, incompatible with life, incompatiblewithlife….

A mistake. It wasn't. They could fix it. No, they couldn't. My son was going to die.

I didn't want to cry. I gripped the sides of the basin in front of me and stared into my own wild eyes and whispered through gritted teeth, "Stop it! Stop. It… Don't."

And then, all at once, I broke. I keened. I sobbed raw, wretched cries, painfully aware that on the other side of the flimsy sliding door my husband and the woman stood awkwardly listening to the sound of a heart breaking.

On the worst day of my life I was ushered into a room in the antenatal clinic and spoke to a nurse about therapeutic termination. I spoke to a doctor who was efficient and kind and explained the process.

This was what was wrong with my son. He had an encephalocele. A severe neural tube defect that made his skull bones fail to fuse. His brain was exposed to the amniotic fluid. He would likely not survive that much longer. He would never survive delivery. He would never take a breath.

The procedure would be a series of pessaries inserted near my cervix to begin labour. After some time, I would give birth. He would be sent for autopsy. They would cremate him. His remains would be interred at the hospital. There was a service once a month for the babies like him. Babies too young to be legally recognised as babies. Babies born before 20 weeks. "You won't have to have a funeral," they said by way of a comfort. As though the fact that his existence could be erased so easily would be a comfort to me.

On the worst day of my life I set a date to come back. We rode home in silence, my swelling stomach a painful reminder of what we were going to lose.

When I came back to the hospital days later I laboured for 7 hours. They offered me morphine because there is no danger to taking drugs when your child will not survive. I refused because I needed to feel everything. My water broke just after 7pm. A midwife came in and delivered the tiniest fairy of a baby you have ever seen. She announced he was a boy. I couldn't bear to look at him so she took him away. The placenta wouldn't shift so I was wheeled to theatre. The shot me full of something that made me sleepy and calm. My face was a blank stone. Tears rolled from my eyes unchecked. A nurse opened the curtains and looked alarmed. "Are you in pain?" She asked. I shook my head, mute and stared at the ceiling. She stepped forward, laid her hand over mine, dry and warm, "Just your heart, hey?" She whispered. My eyes met hers, I gave an imperceptible nod. She gave one back. They put me to sleep.

The next day they brought him to me. His hands and feet bore blue ink from where they had printed them. Someone had made a hood from the blanket so it covered his head. I didn't shift it, not willing to look at the defect that had stolen him from me. I was scared to touch him because I knew he would be cold. I stayed with him a long time. I admired his long feet and tiny toes.

Riley.

We went home. I stayed in bed for three days.

Riley would be almost 18 if he were alive today. If I look at his siblings I can almost patchwork together a picture of how he would have looked. For years after his short time on earth, spent entirely within the safety of my womb where he was nothing but completely loved and wanted, I felt his absence often. Because of who I am I wanted an answer why. I researched everything. I second guessed myself. Two years after his death I called the doctor and she patiently went back over everything with me. The hardest things to deal with is when there is no why.

I met a woman a couple of years later who had recently lost her daughter in the same way I lost Riley. She was the biggest comfort to me, someone who understood completely the Worst Day, who knew the helplessness, the agony. Who else could I explain to that even though he passed away, my sorrow was mixed with a joy, because he had also lived. That what you wanted was not always to brush him away as though he never existed but to talk about him. We passed our children's names to each other and held them like a gift. We could speak freely of regret and sadness and love. I will love her forever for the space she gave me to talk of my son. I hope I gave her some comfort to talk of her daughter.

Now, years later we both have more children. Rainbow babies whose presence in our houses smooth over some of the cracks in our hearts. Children who yell and laugh and dance and sing, and remind us that joy can be had.

You may wonder why the worst day in my life was not the day he left me, the day he was born. The worst day was when I knew I had to give him up, never the day I first saw him, a fleeting glance before the nurse took him away. I could never regret that. Seeing him was one of my best memories, however tinged with sadness.

After Riley when I had my daughter, my rainbow baby, I was overjoyed to be expecting her and yet, I was also scared witless of the whole situation. I barely allowed myself to believe I was pregnant, and at each ultrasound – for her pregnancy there were many – I anxiously watched the screen until I could see her head and traced the perfect roundness of it with my eyes. I told no one I was pregnant until I was absolutely sure she didn't share her brother's fatal condition, and almost as though my body was conforming to my fears, I went off to the 20-week ultrasound not showing at all despite being in a fitted sundress and still I had told no one I was even pregnant. It was only after that all clear and because, due to summer, I could no longer hide it, I finally told family I was having a baby girl. She turned out to be my easiest pregnancy, no morning sickness, none of the ailments I would suffer from in subsequent pregnancies and at 38 weeks, she came into the world after only 2.5 hours of labour. Still, I suffered. I chose the birth centre because I couldn't bear the thought of going back to that ward where I had delivered my son and I wanted the personal touch of a single midwife who would guide me through each appointment and know my fears before I told her. I delivered her on a birthing stool, my midwife behind me to catch my daughter as she entered the world and when she was born and my wonderful midwife called out joyously, "Oh, she's beautiful. Turn around and look at your little girl!" I found myself paralysed. It was probably only a heartbeat, but for me it felt like eternity. In those seconds, all my fears came rushing towards me and I was terrified to look at her and I realised for the last 9 months I had held my daughter at arms-length, frightened to give myself totally to the idea of her in case it was ripped from me again. In the end, I turned around and looked at her, not because I had overcome my fears but because my midwife was so delighted I would have felt badly for disappointing her if I didn't. I loved her, of course. But it took me many months to trust the universe again, after it had dealt me the cruellest blow I could imagine.

Slowly, over time, she healed my wounds until I could think of Riley without aching, until I could speak of him in the same way all mothers recount the details of their child, telling the children how small his feet were, or how big my stomach was while I was pregnant with him. She healed me until, when her brother arrived 3 years later, I had none of the fear I had with her, so that when he was born, I spun around immediately, and took him in my arms with only gratitude in my heart.

For all the babies who we carry in our hearts, whose mothers and fathers silently sing their name. You were never forgotten.

POSTPARTUM

The morning after I gave birth to my eldest daughter, I woke up to a nurse pushing the curtain away from my bed and cheerfully announcing good morning like she was Mary freaking Poppins. I don't believe anyone likes being woken up by someone overly cheerful. In fact, I would infinitely rather be woken up by someone who slouches into the room, and sighs loudly before looking out the window and saying in a kind of depressed voice, "Well, I guess it's that time again." It makes you feel like it's okay to groan, pull the pillow over your head and complain, and I appreciate people that give you that kind of safe space in the morning. One time when my son was about 8, I came in to wake him up for school and in his sleep addled state he wailed, "Arrrrghh, this is *shit*! You had me do this yesterday!" I was alarmed because I had never heard him swear before but I think in the process of waking he somehow channelled a past life where he was sleep deprived mother. I couldn't even get mad because, honestly? Same.

So, when this nurse came in I kind of hated her a little bit. The good thing about those overly cheerful nurses is that they prepare you for being the mother to a toddler who will lift your eyelid at 5am and shout that the sun is up. I muttered some kind of passably polite greeting back to her and began to gather my things to take a shower.

My whole body was in pain. Never before had I related so strongly to the saying, 'hit by a truck'. Muscles I didn't even know I had ached from the hours I'd spent the day beforehand birthing. I made my way to the shared bathroom and began to inspect the damage. I had bled heavier than I had ever anticipated. During the birthing classes I had attended, the nurse running them had said it would be a heavy flow. This seemed like downplaying flash flooding to 'a bit of rain'. In fact, the bleeding seemed like it should be a 'tools down medical emergency' but instead, it's just another day on the maternity ward. I am not alone in the woeful under preparation for postpartum bleeding. One time on an online mothering forum a woman in our Due in Group asked if we thought one packet of pads was enough for her hospital bag. Second time mothers were like, "Two would be better, but one should be fine for a short stay." After some back and forth we realised she had only bought one packet of pads for her entire postnatal period. Try breaking it to someone that they will be having a six-week period some time and see how it feels to be the harbinger of *that* news.

In the bathroom, I looked down at my stomach with morbid fascination. While you're pregnant your stomach is the clear focal point of your body, announcing your entry to a room before you turn the corner. Regardless of how you feel about the rapid expansion of your waistline during pregnancy, it is in most cases this firm, rounded hump, purposeful and ripe. What my stomach now resembled was something more akin to an empty handbag or a cartoon depiction of a kangaroo's pouch or some equally disturbing imagery. Fear not, first time mothers, this mostly goes down over the next few months. Mostly. If you're fortunate enough to have an older child anywhere between the ages of 2-12 they will let you know that you still have a pooch. A few months after the birth of my youngest son, my then 6-year-old daughter came up to me, prodded me in the stomach and announced, "You're still a little bit fat from the baby, are you, Mummy?" In general, I think it's wise to just accept that your body is different after children. Society seems to have conditioned us to believe that our bodies are a stable entity and that change is something to be feared and halted but the fact is, if you intend to try to get through life looking like you're 25 forever, you are going to be a bitterly disappointed 70-year-old. Luckily, most changes happen slowly enough that we are able to get used to it, the postpartum body however is thrust upon you immediately. A period of adjustment is normal. And despite the fact I had a strange skin appendage, I felt oddly proud of my ability to bend at the middle again when putting on underwear.

While I was pregnant, my boyfriend's mother had told me of a client she had when she was a hairdresser who had the most amazing curly hair and that after she gave birth, her hair was dead straight. She said that her client's mother had gone to visit her in the hospital and walked straight past her own daughter because she didn't recognise her with her hair so drastically different. I'm not sure if her customer was prone to hyperbole or not but since I wasn't sure what to expect in the way of changes, I scanned myself in the mirror. I definitely looked different than I had 9 months beforehand but I think deep down I had expected that I would have some glowing transformation that initiated me into motherhood. That I would be the picture of patience and serenity – goddess-like. Instead it just looked like I'd had a really wild night with a bottle of tequila. But satisfied I was the same person except with dark circles under my eyes and a brand new 'skin pouch', I sat down to pee.

Nowadays women let you know what to expect when peeing, bless them. Back then, no one had thought to mention it to me so imagine my alarm when it felt as though someone had just poured lemon juice on a thousand paper cuts. Feeling guilty for disturbing the entire maternity ward with my screaming the day beforehand, I just gritted my teeth and hissed, "Shiiiiiiit" while my eyes watered. Only then did I notice the helpful sign on the back of the toilet door that suggested leaning forward and touching your toes when urinating to lessen the pain from grazes, tears and stitches. If your stomach is the focal point during pregnancy, then the vagina steals the show for the first few days postpartum. The tears, the stitches, the blood, the swelling, and periodically a midwife will ask to 'check your parts' to ensure everything is healing as it should. You would feel undignified having this happen except for the fact that you lost all dignity during the birth when a whole football team could have wandered through the delivery suite and you wouldn't much have cared.

After a few days, the milk comes in. One thing no one prepared me for and I learned only through first-hand knowledge was the strange experience of suddenly having to 'deal with' your boobs. I had watched with interest as they changed during my first pregnancy, developing a heaviness, the skin near translucent with a roadmap of veins suddenly visible beneath the surface. After birth they became engorged, my shirts suddenly porn star absurd as the fabric strained to contain them. The let-down reflex was another thing that I'd had inadequately described to me, "it's a tingling" they had said at birthing classes. That is nearly true, as it does feel slightly similar to your limb waking up after falling asleep… but only if it was to the tenth power and someone was forcing you to run on it during the pins and needles phase. I was unprepared for the geyser of milk that would shoot forth whenever my infant latched on, many times my baby could not keep up with the flow in the beginning.

When the baby grows older, they become easily distracted feeders. They may pop off to glance around at a loud noise or a newcomer to the room with little care as to your own modesty or your desire to save your shirt from milkstains. One time, when I was feeding one of my daughters, we had a workmate over to the house. I didn't know him that well but since I was firmly in the camp of 'baby's got to eat' I decided to nurse my daughter while we all sat in the lounge room having a cup of tea. I was sitting on a couch at right angles to his and he didn't even notice as she latched on as I had become quite good at being discreet. Just after the let-down however, he let out a booming laugh and my daughter popped off and turned her head to look at him. At this moment, a wayward stream of milk went hurtling in his direction and I clapped my hand over my breast and wondered what to do. I was fairly certain none of the milk landed on him but still, it's an incredible faux pas to be squirting milk at guests. I was left with a decision, either apologise and risk bringing attention to something he may not have noticed, or say nothing and risk him having noticed and now be of the opinion that I think nothing of squirting guests with milk. Do it all the time. Don't even say sorry for it. So, finally I say, "Uhh. Sorry about…you know…squirting you with milk just then."

"What?" he says, confused.

So, he didn't notice. Fantastic.

"Yeah. I was feeding her and she hopped off and it just squirted out towards you and I'm so sorry. It was accidental. I'm not in the habit of shooting milk at people."

He looked at me in amazement, "You mean it just comes out? Like a water gun? God, I'd be shooting that at people all the time!"

At least he took it well.

That morning, my first day after birth, my breasts were only slightly tender but not yet engorged and due to my daughter being whisked away to the SCN and given a feeding tube as soon as she was born, I hadn't yet breastfed her or been asked to express any colostrum. Over the coming days I would fall into a rhythm of hand expressing and then tube feeding my daughter through the nasal gastric tube and learn the routines and procedures of the SCN.

Prior to having children, I had never been in the hospital before and since I had also never had a baby before, I felt somewhat like I had been dropped on an alien planet. None of my reading had given me an insight into having a baby that required special care, of bilirubin levels and the ache of having your daughter so close but not being able to hold her to your chest. It was an incredibly hard period of my life, it's awful having to go home from the hospital and leave your baby behind, waking during the night to pump milk and wondering if they're okay and what nurse is on and hoping it's not the crotchety one. In the mornings, someone would either drive me up to the hospital or I would catch the train, carefully carrying the bottles of milk I had expressed overnight. From the train, I would walk to the hospital, wash my hands and sit beside my daughter, listening to the drone of the radio that was on 24 hours a day and which for some reason, seemed to play the same songs on a loop until I thought if I heard Human Nature one more time I would scream. At dinner time, I would do the process in reverse, bringing home empty bottles and empty arms with a hollow spot in my heart.

Slowly, she graduated to a proper crib and she began to nurse properly and one day we were told it was time for her to 'room-in' with me in a normal ward. This is basically a mock version of what happens in full term, healthy births where you come and stay in the hospital for a day or more while you get use to the demands of a newborn without a nurse sitting in the same room as you 24/7 to assist. It's to help you get the hang of breastfeeding if you need to and to ensure the baby is putting on weight and thriving. It kind of feels like a final exam before you get to graduate to a fully-fledged mother going solo without your L plates. Which is kind of funny for me since I actually wasn't even allowed to drive a car solo yet. The babies are weighed each day and if they've gained enough weight by the next weigh in you get to go home, the nurses jokingly calling after you, "See you next year!"

The day after we had roomed in together, at my daughter's

weigh in, I held my breath as she was placed on the scales, waiting to see if she had gained the required amount. When I saw she had gained nearly twice as much as required I basically did a victory lap around the SCN and the paediatrician, judging my display to be suspicious, insisted on keeping her another night to ensure it wasn't some kind of premature baby version of beginner's luck. But when weigh in rolled around the next day she had made an even higher gain and it was at that point I realised my daughter, despite being less than a month old, had a competitive streak.

I think my experience with my firstborn was what guided me to choose less and less medical based models for childbirth until I had my fifth child at home with a midwife. For a multitude of reasons, I ended up back at the hospital for my last child – for one, my midwife had retired from attending homebirths – but also, I believe it was because I now trusted more in my ability to know what I was doing and to advocate for myself and my child, without a dedicated midwife for continuity of care. I don't think continuity of care can be understated and while we have come a long way since I first gave birth 21 years ago, we still tend to treat birth a bit like an assembly line and you can tell staff are overworked and underappreciated in their calling to guide women and babies safely through the process of birth. I am in two minds when I consider the birthing process because while it is natural and women have been doing it since time began, we are relatively safe in childbirth now, owing in large part to those tireless workers who have created the medical model we have in the western world. It's not a perfect system but it's the best we have and we are safer – for the most part – because of it. But you *will* get pushed through and you will sometimes slip through the cracks if you don't speak up. Learning to speak up will hold you in good stead because at some point in your child's life you may find that you know something is wrong. Something no one else seems to see, but you know. For example, when my middle daughter was in prep, I knew there was something 'going on'. She was part of the first prep group to go through in Queensland and back then prep was still very play based. They had dress ups and play-doh and they did water-play days, but towards the end of the year they began to teach them the alphabet in preparation for grade 1. She just couldn't seem to grasp it. I had had two daughters before her, one for whom learning to read was a bit of a struggle but she plodded on, and one for whom it came naturally and once she learnt all the sounds she took off reading like she had been doing it for years. But my middle daughter wrote most letters backwards when writing her name. Despite me sitting with her patiently pointing out sight words and tacking them up around the house, nothing twigged. Finally, at the end of grade 1, I approached her teacher and said, "Do you think something might be wrong?" She assured me it was perfectly normal for some kids to not get the concept of reading straight away, in her experience those kids who lagged behind generally just caught up around the middle of grade 2, when suddenly everything fell into place. I wanted to be reassured by her words but in my heart, I just knew that wasn't going to happen. I voiced concerns again in grade 2, and again at the beginning of grade 3 when my daughter still couldn't read a lick and was continuing to write even her own name incorrectly. Finally, we paid for private testing in the city, a 4 hour drive for us at the time, and she was diagnosed with dyslexia and suddenly everything made sense. This is not to say that everything changed overnight and my daughter got a nifty pair of coloured glasses and started reading Hemingway (it wasn't until grade 7 that she finally was able to read anything more than the most basic of words) but it gave us the tools to help her get by *without* being able to read. I could give you a bunch of other scenarios exactly like this that have happened in the last two decades, where I have known 'something was up' but been fobbed off initially, until I would put my foot down or find someone who would listen.

When you first have a child, in those hazy days of postpartum life, your instinct is just kicking in and you may find you don't yet trust yourself to listen to that internal voice. You fear that you will be seen as hysterical, which is not an unfounded fear as women throughout time have been told they're hysterical when they're actually just seeing things for how they really are. Or perhaps, like me, you sometimes actually *can* be a little bit hysterical and so you aren't sure if this is just your usual panic or actually something you should be paying attention to. I say, pay attention to it anyway. If you fear something is 'not quite right' with your body postnatally then speak up. If you think your baby isn't latching properly on to the nipple, then don't just grit your teeth through the pain, find a midwife or a lactation consultant or your doctor and tell them. If you've decided breastfeeding actually just isn't for you then firmly state your decision and ask for support to transition to bottles. If you feel deep down there is something not right, shout until someone will listen. I say this because, in our current medical system you may find you see a lot of people and these people might only see you for 10 or 20 minutes. But you are with yourself and your baby all the time. They may miss something small that for you is as glaring as a bullseye on a target. I don't mean to imply that all women get handed some kind of mystical sixth sense when they give birth, that is not the case and sometimes you may find that you miss something too, I'm sure many of my friends knew my son was autistic years before I did. This is not your fault. All I am saying is that if your instinct *does* speak to you, that little nagging voice that sometimes whispers but sometimes grabs a megaphone and yells, listen to it. And make other people listen to it too.

And, if I may be so bold, let me offer you one other piece of advice for your postnatal period…pack snacks. I am a finicky eater and slightly neurotic when it comes to food, I have often said jokingly that I don't eat anything I haven't eaten before which always confuses people who wonder how I eat anything at all. But I would have eaten the ass end of a horse during the time I was in hospital after having a baby. I have never been so famished in my life. My ears would prick to the sounds of the lunch trolley rolling up the hall and I would fall on an egg salad sandwich like a woman possessed. During the hours between dinner and breakfast when I was awake and feeding a baby I would become so hungry that my stomach would virtually howl to be fed. Pack snacks. Pack bananas and muesli bars and apples. Pack more than you think is reasonable and more than you think you will need. Trust me, this is a solid investment.

CHAPTER WHATEVER - I'M TOO TIRED TO REMEMBER

Sleep is one of the biggest concerns for new parents. It's one of the first questions you get asked by friends, family or a well-meaning stranger, "Does he sleep well?" Some people do actually have infants that are the unicorns of the baby world, children that sleep through the night from 6 weeks old and we all hate those parents. I mean, not really. We're mostly just jealous but we do hate them a little. For the rest of us, sleep becomes something nearly mythical, like the tooth fairy, you remember its magic but it just doesn't visit you anymore.

I have this recollection from when I was very small, perhaps a baby even, of my grandfather rocking me to sleep. I was a rather spoilt child, the first grandbaby and for a time I lived in my grandparents' house with my mother and two aunts. I always had a lap to climb into or someone who would listen to my chattering, and I liked to be right in the centre of things. I hated bedtime because it meant that everyone might have fun without me. I distinctly remember waking from a day nap when I was a toddler and hearing everyone's joyful shouts from the pool and being rather miffed they had decided to swim without *me*, as though I expected the world to stop when I slept until I could join it again. I was really a very self-absorbed child. On this particular night, my grandfather was rocking me to sleep and I was crying miserably into his shoulder, exhausted but fighting sleep because the longer I cried the longer he would be required to hold me and give me all his attention. Eventually, after quite a long time of him pacing up and down the hallway singing me lullabies, he got fed up and plonked me on the centre of my mother's bed and left the room, leaving me there shocked at this behaviour from a man who until this point had been nothing but endlessly patient with me my whole life. I remember feeling contrite and saddened even though he soon returned to pick me up and rock me to sleep once again.

It's remarkable the lengths parents go to in order to ensure their infants sleep. We rock them for hours, sing them made up songs, drive the car around the block repeatedly and threaten bodily harm to doorknockers who unsuspectingly ring the doorbell after you've just gotten the baby down. Children, for their part, can be jerks sometimes when it comes to sleep. They don't mean to be, just as I didn't mean to be when I forced my poor grandfather after a full day's work to walk the hallway with me for hours, but they can be, nonetheless. I must have walked kilometres around my lounge room with my middle daughter. She completely rocked my confidence in my ability to be a mother at all. Lulled by her relatively easy pregnancy and uncomplicated birth, I mistakenly thought she was going to be a breezy child. For the first two days in the birth centre she slept contentedly, feeding appropriately and looking around at intervals taking in the sights of the world. I am now fairly sure she was just conserving energy so she didn't have to sleep at all for the next 6 months. I remember saying in great shock, "They're not usually like this." And for years after I joked that if she had been my first, she would have been my last. Somewhere around the 4 month mark I was walking the lounge room in the dark, remembering all the sleep I had gotten prior to kids with something akin to lust, when I slowly rocked down on to the arm of the chair and hoped she wouldn't notice I was no longer pacing. She immediately began fussing and finally I switched on the radio to get some company that wasn't the sounds of my small daughter's cries. She slept. She slept to the sounds of Jimmy Barnes singing about how he left his heart to the sappers 'round Khe Sanh. For the next two months, the only way she would sleep at night was if Jimmy was telling stories about working class men and flame trees and, while I appreciate Barnesy is somewhat of an Australian icon, I eventually found a CD of more infant appropriate music that she would sleep to. For two years whenever we travelled we had to do it with a CD player and 'her music' or I would get no sleep at all.

I say, do whatever you have to, with what you have at the time. Everyone will have some advice for you and some you will decide is useful and some of it will leave you wanting to claw the eyes out of the person who gave it. Both these reactions are normal, don't be so hard on yourself, you're surviving on 4 hours sleep after all. If you decide sleep school is a good idea then go ahead and do that. And if you decide you need to co-sleep then give that a crack too. People will tell you that if you co-sleep then you'll never get the child out of your bed but I assure you that my 19-year-old definitely doesn't want to climb into bed beside me and hasn't for many years. When my second son was born he had a little swollen eye as though he had whacked it on my pelvic bone on the way out, like someone might walk into a doorframe, and as a result, he snored. The snoring didn't bother me, I liked the little *hink-shoo* he did with each breath, but it drove my husband to distraction and he eventually got up and slept in the other bed. We both discovered that this sleeping arrangement suited us just fine and for the next year we slept in separate beds while I co-slept with the baby. We just did whatever worked for us; he got to have a decent sleep and I got the whole king-size to myself, win-win. Or maybe not, since we divorced some years later but I'm quite sure that wasn't a result of sleeping separately for 12 months, whatever. The point is, do what works, leave what doesn't, and attempt to get some sleep as best you can.

Eventually, the early days wane and despite your chronic sleep deprivation, you begin to get a grip on this thing called parenthood. Your child begins to interact with you more, smiling with a fierce joy that reaches their eyes, crinkling at the corners and eventually they will give you a little hiccup like laugh, startling in its arrival. For the first year everything goes so fast that you barely have time to settle into one routine before it goes and changes on you and that never happens so fast as when they begin to move.

Children are remarkable in their tenacity to get somewhere. At first you encourage them, clapping with pride when they roll over as though they've just graduated dux of the school. Then you realise you made a terrible error. Even before they can get up on all fours and crawl, they will dig their little toes into the floor and scoot along the ground on their stomach leaving you with a bunch of rompers where the front looks like the bottom of your mop. If you ever want to know how dirty your floors are, just pop a commando crawling baby on the floor and see what happens to their clothes. Not only that, but you now realise your house is full of danger. In fact, it's a wonder any of you are alive at all. If you have older children then this becomes even more magnified as they drop everything like Hansel and Gretel through the house and leave behind them a wake of choking hazard like Lego and dress up jewellery. I truly believe if you ever lose anything in your house, just let lose a crawling child and before you know it, they'll have found the item and put it in their mouth. They love remotes, phones, keys, coins, but if you try to feed them mashed organic pumpkin they'll act like you've just fed them a spoonful of arsenic. My second son ate paint, washing powder crumbs that had fallen on the floor, cat biscuits, dirt. I joked with my Nanna that I had poisons control on speed dial. He was remarkably fast for one so small and I came to believe he would formulate a plan for how to find whatever thing he shouldn't have and then put the plan into action the moment I left the room, like Catherine Zeta-Jones in Entrapment. One time, before he was scarcely able to stand I left him in the lounge room to grab nappy changing items and was gone for ten minutes and when I came back he was sitting on the computer chair banging away at the keys. I thought that was a bit cheeky and marvelled at how he had managed to climb up there. I picked him up and realised his nappy was totally drenched. My first instinct was to think he had urinated straight through it but there was so much liquid this seemed unlikely. Slowly, a realisation dawned on me and I looked at the turtle tank, which was now suspiciously murky. In the ten minutes I had been out of the room, my son had pushed the computer chair over to the tank, threw the turtle out, had a good splash, got down, and wheeled it back to the computer and was cheerfully smiling at me. The turtle was found shaken but otherwise well on the floor. You can't tell me that act wasn't premeditated, he was a genius who was using his powers for evil. It had honestly never occurred to me to secure the turtle away before that moment, it was on a sturdy stand over 3-foot-high, I was gone for 10 minutes, but infants are determined little creatures.

Another thing that happens when you have a baby is you suddenly find yourself tracking someone else's bowel movements. One minute you're having a nice dinner with your partner and the next you're out to lunch (because dinner is too late and you need to put the kids to bed) and you find you're in a deep discussion over the salad about your child's bowel motions. If you are breastfeeding, doctors, nurses and the well-meaning stranger on the internet will tell you anything goes. They may go daily, they may not go for a week, don't worry. Formula fed babies are meant to be a bit more regular. And once solids starts, forget all the rules, there are new ones. I remember my second Christmas as a mother. We had decided to hold a lunch at our house as it was the first Christmas since my father in law had died and I don't think any of us could bear to sit in my mother in laws house without him, so we decided it would be at our place. My second daughter was 5 months old at the time and we also had a six-month-old border collie puppy and if you look up the definition of insanity in the dictionary there will be a picture of me with two children under two and adding a puppy into the mix. For the most part, he was a good and obedient dog but he had recently discovered a hole in the fence that if he tried very hard he could squeeze through. We had patched it up though and so far, he seemed to be thwarted in his escape attempts.

My daughter had recently started solids and this had played havoc with her bowels and we were 6 days with no movement and one extremely cranky baby. People love to tell you how to fix your child's bowels. If you ever want to know whether folklore is alive and well in modern times, just tell someone your child is constipated and they'll have you walking 20 steps backwards under the full moon or other such nonsense. As such, I found myself on Christmas Eve with a thousand things to do, sitting on the floor, giving my child a little bit of brown sugar in water and massaging her stomach in a clockwise motion while intermittently cycling her legs. Because of the massage her nappy was undone and she kicked her legs happily, enjoying the freedom.

Suddenly, I see a black and white blur run past the window and down the street and I realise the dog has gotten out again. I yell out down the house that I am off after the dog and without waiting for a response I take off down the street after a pup that's hell bent on enjoying every second of his ill-gotten freedom. I doubt I ever would have caught him if he hadn't decided to stop and pee on every light post but after about ten minutes I wrangle the dog into the backyard, McGyver a fix for the fence, and give the dog a stern talking to about running off when I'm busy trying to have some Christmas cheer, goddammit. I come back inside the house and the baby is now in the kitchen. She wasn't yet crawling but she could manage to wiggle worm her way along and get where she needed to go. *And* she wasn't constipated anymore. She had left a trail behind her like a snail which let me know that before making it into the kitchen she had rolled all around the lounge room floor after making it off her change mat and the play quilt underneath. And that was how I ended up shampooing my carpets the day before Christmas.

Try to take help wherever you can get it. Sometimes you will have to ask for it because people worry that if they offer they will be offending you or because you look like you really have it together – but only because they haven't seen you when you turn up to the bus stop to collect your kids wearing baby upchuck on your shirt. One time I was in the shops on my own and when I went to pay for my groceries at the check-out, there was a woman there who had a tiny baby squalling in the trolley as she tried to quickly load her groceries onto the conveyor. I had once been that mother with only two arms who was trying to do three things at once who desperately needed a hand. However, I had also been the mother getting stares from passer-by's who whispered under their breath while my toddler melted down in the aisle and I juggled a newborn in my arms. I desperately wanted to offer my assistance but I didn't want to come off as though I was judging her or have her think that I was merely offering because she seemed incapable. After some internal dialogue, I went over and asked if she would like me to either hold her baby or put her groceries up for her. She looked at me in that way that mother's do when their mind is actually thinking of a hundred other things. You can almost see the computer churning behind their eyes as they run through grocery lists and appointments and they answer you without really seeing you, mostly so that you will go away and it's one less thing that they will have to deal with. "Oh! No. Thank you, but I'm fine."

I smiled at her and went on my way, glad I had offered help but wishing I could sit her down for a cuppa and a piece of cake and rock her baby while she decompressed for ten minutes. I wanted to tell her that I had been there, that I had once been so tired I had walked the entire markets with my shirt inside out and only realised when I stopped to feed my son and noticed the facing of my shirt pressing up against his cheek. I wanted to tell her about how I once grocery shopped daily for six months, not because I enjoyed it but because I could only manage the brain power to think of one day's worth of meals at a time. Trust me, people get it. Even when you think you're the only person who's ever dry shampooed their hair for a week because you haven't had time to wash it, you really aren't.

Of course, babies are delicious. That's mostly why we don't take them back to the hospital for a refund, because honestly, they're messy and loud and if they were your friends – they wouldn't be. But they're also funny and cute and there is nothing quite so amusing as when a small person in a fluffy onesie is trying to look indignant about something. I have so many little videos of my youngest daughter when she was tiny and she's really doing nothing in them, just laughing as the cat plays with a piece of ribbon or sleeping or sneezing and I know I shot that because I thought it was just the most incredible thing I'd ever seen. It is probably the photographer in me telling you this, but take photos. Take so many photos that you're embarrassed about how many you have. And I don't mean professional photos, although absolutely take those too, but take the photos about nothing. Take the ones where they've got Vegemite toast all over their face or the one where they're intrigued by a piece of grass. Take the ones where they have half their foot shoved in their mouth or the one where they've gotten into the washing basket and are wearing your bra as a hat. Sometimes it can feel as though you will never survive that first year, but just remember transition and know you will, or, as one of my friends once told me about a time in my life when I was very worried and overthinking everything, just be in the now. When they're finally asleep and you look down into your arms and notice the way their lashes curl over their cheek, be in the now. Because it all does go by so fast. I know that can be frustrating to hear, and it's usually old ladies at the supermarket that come over and tell you it. And you smile and nod but repress the urge to scream because you've only had 12 hours sleep in 4 days and you found yourself eating peanut butter out of the jar, and you can't imagine a time where you would ever long for these days. But really what those ladies are doing is remembering their own babies and the joy they had when they held them and how the miss the weight of their children in their arms who are all off living their own lives. So, when that happens, go home and ignore the washing and lie down on the floor with your child and just be in the now.

Another lesson on what is really important was given to me by my father in law before he died. I was 6 weeks pregnant with my second daughter when we lost him to Lymphoma. He was a family man, clever, gentle yet fiercely protective, he smiled right up until the day he died. He spent almost the entire first year of my eldest daughter's life in and out of hospital as he went through the rigors of chemotherapy and a bone marrow transplant and all the other hundreds of medical procedures that go with cancer. When he was in hospital, my mother in law put photos of the family in his room. Some of them had my daughter in the garden, in a little bonnet while she plucked grass out of the lawn and probably ate a good portion of it. In the times where he was home he would dote on my daughter, carrying her until she fell asleep. I remember one time, he gave her a little white chocolate frog and held her while she ate it. She was drooling all down the shoulder of his sweater, this messy chocolatey goo and I was mortified and tried to take her off him to save his shirt. He stopped me and said, "It doesn't matter, Missy. It's just a shirt." But he held my eyes for a moment and I knew he was telling me about something more than just clothing. Because it was true. It really *doesn't* matter. Clothing will wash, but holding his granddaughter, well…that was priceless. He did that often for me in the last few months, say something seemingly simple and then he would hold my gaze or squeeze my hand, to tell me to remember this and to take it to heart because he was speaking with his. And I do. I remember all those little gifts of wisdom and about not sweating the small stuff. His death was the first time I had really had to confront human mortality up close and personal and while he was taken too soon and not much older than I am now, he died surrounded by family, his wife literally singing him to heaven. Because family really is the very most important thing. And everything goes by too fast.

14th of June 2019 – The Journals

Sometimes when I am driving to work I look at the mountains down the long straight road and I imagine I am sending snapshots of my life to a past me. Photos taken with my eyes. I sent it to a 16 year old me, or a 25 year old me, a 30 year old me, or even me from 12 months ago.

I send these photos and I imagine what they would think or say about that. I send 16 year old me a photo of my daughter curled fast asleep in my arms. I send a photo of me driving my car to work, a cardigan demurely buttoned, long sleeved to cover my tattoos, to 25 year old me. I send a photo of my study to 30 year old me and then I notice the cockerspaniel statues painted by my mum and Nanna (that I always said was the only thing I wanted when they passed) and I worry she will think they have died so I scrawl a note saying they are alive and I send that too.

When I feel like I am drowning in responsibilities, like I have fallen behind, I send out these snapshots of my life and I feel a past me cheering me on. I know that even if my life looks different to what she supposed it might, she would be accepting of it, excited by it, proud of me. See, I never really had expectations of myself. I never really believed in me. I never thought I could leave the house and have a life. We are always told to look forward but I find my biggest comforts come from looking back.

I am fragile at the moment. I can feel the cracks along my surface and I know I am walking on a knife's edge. The only difference is that I have been here before. I am not fearful of falling because even if I do, I can pull myself out. Life is not comfortable. It's raw. I run my hands along my scars and I cherish them for they mean that I am healed. I used to think healing meant you were better. I thought it meant you would go back to who you were before any of this happened to you. But healing means that you are changed. But you're okay. I'm okay. We're going to be okay

THE DARKNESS

Twice in my life I've been so depressed and anxious I was half worried I would die. The other half of me was worried I *wouldn't* die and that this would just be my life now and both scenarios were equally horrifying for me. The first time was just after I gave birth to my second eldest daughter, but in hindsight I think it began when I was pregnant with her. I've spent a long time autopsying my depression to try to find the cause, I've gone over it carefully, turning it over in my hands and searching for why. The truth is, I don't know. What I know is that one day when I was pregnant, I took my daughter to the library, pushing her in her pram and on the way home I suddenly felt like I was going to have a heart attack, or pass out, or throw up, or some combination of the three. I sat down, right there on the pavement and took deep gulping breaths but nothing helped. Eventually, when I made it home I went and laid down for half an hour and then I felt quite alright. But the damage was done. Whenever I went to go out the door my body screamed danger and I shut it again. I was a depressed agoraphobic with social anxiety and it was crippling.

. . .

After my daughter was born, I thought all of that would go away, like morning sickness. But instead it magnified. Finally, I called Lifeline, who had me hold the line while they contacted the mental health unit at the hospital, who arranged for a social worker to visit me the following day. I was so sick when she came that I couldn't get out of bed. So, she came and sat on the foot of it. For a whole week, she came daily and sat at the foot of my bed and she brought in a psychologist and he sat at the foot of my bed too. At the end of the week I made it to the couch and she cheered like I'd just done something really impressive and I felt jacked off that my life had been reduced to people cheering because I'd managed to drag my sorry ass out of bed. For a year and a half, I saw my social worker, at first every day and then three times a week and then finally once a week. I saw more psychologists and psychiatrists than I can count and I'm sure I sounded incredibly off kilter which, to be honest, I was a little.

I felt pursued by a darkness, hunted, even as I tried to shake it off and find my way out. It was almost like every single unresolved feeling I had ever had was lining up to be heard and agonised over. Sometimes I just lay on the floor, as though sitting up was committing too much to life. Sometimes I got a wild urge to run, as though if I just charged out the door I wouldn't have time to be haunted by it. As though if I ran and kept running I could outpace the shadows. I wish I could describe it to you, *really* describe it. I've lived with it for so long now that it feels like it's too woven into the fabric who I am for me to see it accurately and pull out the words to tell you, it's like trying to taste your own tongue. All I can say is that I was really very, very sick. I think part of the reason I kept going over every terrible feeling I had ever had was because I was trying to find which one might be responsible for the way I currently felt and when that one would come up empty, I'd pick up the next one.

When I was in labour with my fourth child, my eldest son, I didn't know I was in labour. I had gone to my GP that day to complain about my Symphysis Pubis Dysfunction and she became alarmed at the pain I was in and wrote a letter for me to take up to the hospital to be induced. In hindsight, I can see that no one at the hospital would have cared, that SPD was just a fact of life for some women but at the time it felt very important and official having a letter from one's GP. We waited a long time to be seen and the room we sat in had a clock. Periodically my uterus would tighten but without any real pain and after a couple of hours staring at that clock I realised the tightenings were happening every 10 minutes, almost on the dot. I tentatively mentioned it to my husband who became very excited and finally we made it into the room and my midwife from the birthing centre came in looking tired, harried and not just a little cranky. She brushed aside my concerns about contractions and told me the medical version of 'cowgirl up' about the pain of the SPD. We left the hospital.

At home I took a shower, drowned my sorrows in some take away and cocooned myself in my dressing gown, morose. The pains kept coming and they began to hurt. I kept taking showers, the heat on my back was the only thing that seemed to ease the pains and finally, reluctantly, I called the hospital at about 7pm to say I thought maybe I was having contractions. The hospital put me on hold and called my midwife who told them I was not in labour, she had already seen me 5 hours ago. The midwife on the other end relayed this in a way that made me think she didn't like my midwife very much. She told me to call back if my water's broke or if the pain got worse. I got off the phone and I cried. My husband went to sleep. I tried to go to sleep but found myself unable to lie still. I was on all fours at the bottom of the bed, rocking and panting. I got up and took yet another shower. And when it came to 1am I again called the hospital, this time full of apologies. The same midwife listened and waited patiently as I huffed and panted unable to speak while another pain gripped me tightly. Then she said, "Do you think you should come in?"

"I don't know!" I wailed, "My midwife says I'm not in labour!"

And she replied, "Honey? If you can't talk through the contractions, then it sounds like you're in labour."

Even then I second guessed myself. *Could* I talk through the contractions? Maybe I could if I really tried. But I woke my husband anyway and we put the bags in the car and began driving to the hospital, the highway empty of cars, it felt like we were the only people in the world.

When you arrive at the main entrance of the hospital in the wee hours of the morning, it is shut. You have to press the intercom button and inform the security guard what is going on and he comes out and lets you in. So, my husband presses the button and when asked what is happening my husband answers, "My wife is in labour." And I suffered from terrible guilt that we had just lied to the security guard and would be passing him again in an hour when they informed me I was the world's biggest hypochondriac.

. . .

Upstairs they led me to a room and the sweet midwife from the phone met me cheerfully and said she was going to give me an exam. She felt around for a moment, looked up at me and smiled, "8cms," she announced, then busied herself readying the room muttering unkind things about my midwife who she hoped wouldn't arrive in time and that would serve her right. You could have knocked me over with a feather. I nearly cried in relief at the validation of it. As it was, it went fairly slowly from there, he wasn't born until 5am and my cranky midwife had plenty of time to catch my son, who arrived looking like a little wizened raisin.

Even fourth time around, someone else's doubt made me lose confidence in my body and what I knew was happening. I had all these doubts transferred to me and felt like I was being a waste of everyone's time. In fairness, I had never had labour start like that, with my first two births my water had broken first and the third was induced and each time I was already assured the contractions were real but this time I had to go on blind faith in my own body. On intuition. So many times as a mother you will have to trust in yourself, which is so hard because you are existing on 3 hours of broken sleep and you haven't showered in two days and you smell like sour milk and neurosis. You feel lonely and you also hate everyone and want them to go away. It's disconcerting to realise that while the world has totally shifted on its axis for you, for everyone else it's just a normal Wednesday. You aren't sure what you're doing but you're fairly certain you're doing it wrong, so how can you be trusted to know if what is going on is real? For women, this is a big deal. Almost every woman I know has a story of going to the doctors with an ailment and being fobbed off. Some of us are timid creatures who will slink away, ashamed to have wasted the good doctors time. Some of us are more vocal but even those who of us who usually roar can be stunned into silence by the exhaustion, the shock of birth and new parenting.

Constantly women are told to speak up if they feel like they are slipping into the darkness of depression after a baby. There are three reasons this may not happen. The first is what I described above, the feeling that you will be told you're wrong and you don't want to be a bother to anyone if you're wrong which you feel you probably are because just that morning you put the baby's nappy on backwards and didn't even notice. The next is that you don't see it coming. Have you ever been reading in the late afternoon and you're going along just fine, wondering what will happen next to the protagonist when someone says something or the dog barks and you look up and realise that the sun has set some time ago? You look back down to the page which you could see clearly just a moment ago but it's all in shadow, there is no way you could read it now. Sometimes depression is like that. You think you're doing okay and then all of a sudden you realise the light has been fading for a really long time. And then what happens once your there? Which brings me to the third reason, it's too much. It's too big. When you are struggling to survive it's unreasonable to expect that person to also make a plan and employ that plan to save themselves. We don't shout to drowning people to simply figure it out themselves. We toss them a lifesaver and we pull them in. We dive in after them. So, before you have your baby nominate someone to check in on you. Nominate several people actually. Be selective and pick people you know will care, those who will help, pick those who would dive in after you. Tell them to keep an eye on you, to text you to ask if you're okay, or invite you out for a coffee and see how you are doing. And be that person for someone else.

I would like to tell you that I got well. But I didn't really ever 'overcome' the social anxiety. I manage it. And that is a large distinction to make. I still have triggers that set me off into a downward spiral but I have collected a little arsenal of things that help, and sometimes they work and sometimes they don't, but I live with it and manage it as best I can. If you've ever experienced depression or anxiety, or if you currently live with it and, like me, will probably have it tagging along for the rest of your life like some unwelcome, inoperable tumour, then I don't need to tell you what it's like - you get it.

What I want to talk to you about is not how I got well and I'm not going to give you advice on how *you* can get well because I'm barely qualified to handle my own problems. What I'm going to tell you about is tenacity. I'm going to tell you about a warrior. Some time ago, I had a relapse and it was pretty ugly. I spent many hours awake before dawn, with my anxiety for company, watching the sun rise…which all sounds very nice except I was actually vomiting from the anxiety at the time. I retreated to bed. I couldn't get up. My boyfriend at the time came over and brought me flowers because he was scared of my fragility and he loved me and he probably thought he was going to find me in the bathroom cutting off all my hair. He also hoped it would tempt me to get out of bed and put them in a vase and he was hoping to coax me into making the small trip to the kitchen. So, he placed the flowers on the end of the bed and kissed me and then left. I wanted to get up, I really did. But I just couldn't. It took me a week to be well enough to start doing the school run again. And then it took many therapists visits for my mental state to be more robust than rice paper. So, what I did during that period is I wrote. I put down all the horrible, embarrassing parts of my illness and I sent them out into the internet and my friends read it and I thought I would be totally mortified except so many of them sent me messages and said, "Me too." And what I realised after a couple of months was not that I was fragile but that I was strong. I realised that despite the fact that I was so sick I was waking in the morning and vomiting with anxiety, I was still fighting to be well. I was fighting so hard. And when I was feeling like I just couldn't go on, when I was sitting on the floor of the shower and crying, there was a part of me that would say, "Get up." That would refuse to let me give in. A little internal cheer-leader hell-bent on forcing me to live.

I also learned people are kind. My friends reached out to me and would message me or text me, my family would call me, and my boyfriend kept buying me flowers. And with each of those tiny little acts, they lit a torch for me in the darkness, to guide my way home.

Undated 1999 – The Journals

Where does the child go
 When all you feel is lost
 When you have to grow up
 No matter what the cost...

ON BEING A TEENAGE MOTHER

*P*erhaps because I was so young when I had my first, the first couple of years felt like I was trying on different hats, trying to figure out who I was in this world now. When I first took my daughter home it felt like an achievement in and of itself. After two weeks in the SCN, this was graduation. For myself though, I wasn't quite sure where I fit within the world now. I was still too young to drive, vote, sign a contract without my mother signing as a guardian. My peers, whom I had mostly drifted away from, were still in school, taking tests and doing homework. There wasn't really anyone to ask for advice this time as everyone I knew who had children had already become someone first, they had a job to go back to or a plan in place. I was becalmed.

For years, up until I was in my late 20's even, I would dream about being in the classroom. It was exactly as I left it, all the people the same, I would be in English or Drama, or even Maths and I would look at the clock and remember my children. Always, I was trying to leave to go and get them from wherever they were in my dream, day-care, or a babysitter. I would be rushing through the rabbit's warren of paths, trying to find the exit, being held up by friends or teachers as I tried to get to my car to get to the children, my bag hitting my legs as I ran, my books spilling from my arms. I would feel this panic that I wouldn't make it in time as I was being pulled in two different directions. And then I would wake, frightened and panting until I remembered where I was, that school was long over, that my children were safe in their beds. I think that was what being a teenage mother was like. A lack of closure on one part of your life so that the door stood ajar and you found yourself constantly bumping into it as you went about your life. There is a constant warring inside you as you try to regain some semblance of who you were and discover who you *are*, while also wanting to be the very best parent you could be to these small people whom you love with your whole heart.

I was seven when my grandfather taught me to ride a bike. It was this old one he had rescued from my great grandparent's place and he had painted it silver and he set it down on the long concrete driveway and for days we went back and forth, me peddling while he held on to the back, running after me and holding me steady. "Don't let go," I would say over and again. And he would assure me he wouldn't. Until one day I was up the bottom of the driveway and he laughed, "You're doing it!" and I turned around and saw him cheering me from the other end. That's what it's like when you're raising teenagers. You hold on to the back of the seat until finally you let go one day and they're riding on their own. My mother wasn't strict but she wasn't overly relaxed either. She still held the reins though and prior to finding out I was going to be a mother I still had to ask my *own* mother if I could go sleep at a friend's house. I still got *pocket money*. Suddenly, I had to make all the decisions. For a teenage parent, there are no training wheels and no coach holding the back of the seat and you have no choice but to stay upright because your baby is on the bike too.

When I was doing research for this memoir amongst my own journals and notes from over the years, I came across a journal I had written when I was 18. I was searching for a particular poem I had written about postnatal depression because I wanted to find out the exact way I had described what I was going through because sometimes unless you're in the darkness yourself, it's very hard to imagine, even if you've been there before. And also, I think, because depression makes the days blend into one another and afterwards remembering your feelings is like trying to recall a dream, everything is soft around the edges. People have asked me a few times, usually around my eldest daughter's birthday, what it was like to be a teenage mother. I often say it wasn't all that different to when I became a mother to my youngest at 29, because the love is the same. People, many people, were kind to us. I don't remember anyone being mean or saying anything really horrible. Most of the time though, I guess it's not what people say but the look they get in their eyes, because few people can hide their feelings in their face, even when they think they're doing a stellar job. But when I opened this journal and read it, I realised how much I had forgotten.

I talk about my fears about getting married, that I didn't feel ready but that I didn't want to disappoint anyone. I talk about how I felt like if I didn't get married I would be one more teenage girl who got pregnant and then didn't stay with the father of their baby. I talked about the mourning of my youth and the fear that I had disappointed my mother who I knew wanted the best for me. I talked about my insecurities about my body and my sexuality and how I wanted to travel and how I wanted to go back to school but I was too scared to try. I talked about how much the death of my father in law had affected me and how much we all missed him. I poured all of this out in bits and pieces, stilted paragraphs I must have written between changing nappies and feeding babies. And in the margins, was maths, power bills I had due and how much money I had in my bank account and where I could cut a cost that week. My deepest adolescent thoughts sitting side by side with my adult responsibilities. It was painful to read. I actually tore several pages out and ripped them into tiny pieces and put them in the bin immediately because they were agony. Perhaps over the coming weeks I will rip out the rest and maybe have a little bonfire and burn up all those horrible things that girl thought about herself because I'm not her anymore.

I spoke in that journal about wishing I could put it all down in a manuscript and on one page I had begun to write it, just a few lines and then the rest of the page is blank and I wonder now why I stopped, what called me away and made me abandon it. If nothing else, I am grateful that I'm doing that now. I wish I could show her it and tell her she raised some really wonderful young adults, that even though she had no idea what she was doing and felt like she was winging it, she did okay. Luckily, I've always done my best work under pressure.

Undated 2002 – The Journals

She has bronzed skin from swimming and her hair is almost pure white. I think she would smell like sunshine. Her laugh is so clear and pure as it splits the morning, so real that you can almost see it reach up through the trees to the birds. She has skinned knees from tripping over the dog and the remnants of a long eaten peach around her mouth which makes me think I should grab a cloth and wipe her face but I don't want to disturb her while she is playing so nicely. She pumps her legs as she swings, higher and higher and the dog barks in alarm, before losing interest to follow a bug.

I remember that feeling of swinging, the way the wind would rush past you and the slight thump of the swing-set when you got too high and I wish I could freeze this moment. Where she still believes she can touch the sky if she swings high enough, catch a rainbow, carry a cloud in a jar. She sings sweetly, a song from a cartoon, in a voice untrained and off-key, "You can't take me, 'cause I'm free! I'm free!"

LITTLE

For my 37th birthday I got given a FitBit. That sounds like one of those gifts that are an insult in disguise, like getting your overweight friend a gym membership that they never asked for. But I genuinely did want the Fitbit because I'm a slight hypochondriac and it feeds my neurosis to see my heartrate whenever I like. Also, as a photographic editor I would spend 8 plus hours a day sitting at a desk living on cola and crackers and having something remind me to move might be a good thing or at least stop me getting varicose veins because honestly, I'm a little vain about my legs. In not too long I was sick of those little FitBit reminders. There I was, trying to smash out 600 photos in an hour, in the hope of improving my hourly wage (the only person more broke than a starving artist is their editor) and my wrist would vibrate and the FitBit would start nagging me to take some steps. I'd try to sit down and eat a sandwich and it would complain. I would cozy up with a book and my crochet and *buzz* – there it went again. This is exactly what having a small child is like. Anytime you are in the middle of something – *buzz*! They want juice. *Buzz*! They need their colouring pens. *Buzz*! They've woken from their nap after only 20 minutes. It's such a good tool for teaching you to deal with constant interruption and irritation that I think they should give them out to all prospective parents at birthing classes. I think I personally reached peak interruption when my son interrupted me in the middle of birthing his brother and there I was - at 8cms dilated, panting while resetting a Tamagotchi – there really are no boundaries.

And even as they ask you for everything under the sun, they also demand to do everything themselves. This usually only extends to anything that will be messy, difficult or dangerous. You become used to the words, "I do it!" because your toddler believes they are capable of functioning as a fully-fledged adult even while they are calling out for you to wipe them after they've used the potty. With my eldest daughter, I felt like we were constantly caught in a battle of wills because I knew that I was correct when I said that she couldn't pour a cup of milk from a full 2L bottle and I was sure if I explained it she would see the logic and perhaps respond with, "You're right, Mummy. If I pour this out I *will* spill it all over the floor. Here, you had better do this."

Instead she would throw herself down on the floor as though she were felled by an invisible arrow and wail at the injustice. I heard a tip about washing out the squeeze lids from sauce bottles and attaching them to the milk bottle to reduce flow when held upside down, which is great in theory but in reality, just means your child has really impressive length when shooting milk across the room. By the time I had my sixth child and she insisted on putting jam on her own toast, I just handed her the jar and a butter knife and stood there while she lathered more and more jam on to the bread until it disappeared. And finally, when she had 2cms of jam on her piece of toast I sat her at the table, smiled sweetly and told her I hope she enjoyed her breakfast. She did not (although the chickens did) and then I was 'allowed' to make her jam toast from then on. A good portion of dealing with a toddler is psychological warfare.

When I had my youngest daughter, I knew she would be my last and so I tried to savour every moment of her as though if I soaked in all the memories they would seep into me and become a part of who I was. As though I would be able to carry the feeling of her cheek against my arm as I cradled her and the smell of the crown of her head with me for the rest of my life. I thought almost everything she did was wonderful. She was probably the most doted on child in the world, with five older siblings who would carry her around like a trophy, showing her their toys, bouncing her carefully on the trampoline, introducing her to the chickens and goats. The goats would snuffle at her hair, pressing their warm soft noses into her little hands and make her laugh with a pure joy. She became this little person almost immediately, from the time she could smile we tried to get little belly laughs out of her and we would be silly and sing her made up songs and sometimes she would half smile at us and give us this singular little snort like when someone thinks you're amusing only because you're ridiculous. Sometimes it felt like she was a little old man trapped in the body of a tiny girl. Other times though she would just be a sweet baby, who was delighted by helium balloons and pushing over block towers she would have us build. And as she got older she became bossy and independent and sometimes she would act silly purely so she could make us laugh, just as we did for her. But because she was still really only a very tiny girl she could still sometimes be irrational. One time I found her crying morosely because she was trying to shove a barbie shoe on to her foot. This was almost as bad as when my eldest daughter once pitched a full on screaming fit because she wanted me to put the shoes from a catalogue 'on her feet'. There I am trying to explain that you can't put a 2-dimensional item that's roughly 1cm long onto size 4 feet and wondering what I was doing with my life.

Toddlers will do things that make you worry they'll be on YouTube fail video one day and question whether that cup of coffee you had when you were pregnant may have affected them developmentally. They seem to have no sense of their own mortality when they climb to the top of toys they've precariously stacked to reach the thing they shouldn't have, when they scoff dog biscuits like gourmet treats, when they shove things up their nose. Alas, I was just the same.

When I was little I had a beaded purse that I occasionally carried around and tried to fill with coins by begging money from my relatives like a panhandler. I remember one day, having just gone down to my grandfather in his workshop and receiving a small treasure worth of silver coins from his pockets, one of the beads came loose from the threads and into my chubby little four-year-old hand fell an orange bead, about half the size of a pea. I rolled it in between my fingers and felt like I had received a gift. I glanced around to see if anyone was in sight and then… I put it up my nose. Even as I did it I knew it was a bad idea but I was compelled to do it anyway. My daughter calls the compulsion to do things you know you shouldn't, 'the call of the void'. It's like how my grandfather use to say that he couldn't stand near the edge of a cliff because he was worried he would suddenly fling himself off. Once the bead was in my nose the spell was broken and I began to panic, shooting it out with a forceful blow that sent it skittering across the floor, lost, never to be found again. So, when my children came to me crying with things jammed up their nose, I can't even be cross, I just sigh and set about trying to retrieve it. In most instances, it can be worked out without much trouble, although my middle daughter did once stick a wad of playdoh up there that was significantly more difficult to extract. (Pro tip, eventually the snot lubricates the doh and it slides right out. Gag, and then dispose.) And when my eldest son was 3, he broke into his sister's jewellery box and found several small gem stones and proceeded to shove them as far up his nostril as he could. I tilted him backwards and shone a light up there, marvelling, "How many did you put up there?"

His sisters began fighting over whose gemstones they were.

"If it's a red one, it's mine!"

"NO! You had the green one, the red one belongs to me."

"Well, if it's blue then it's mine."

"Girls! Do you mind? I have your brother here with a foreign object lodged in his face, can we maybe wait to fight until *after* I've gotten it out?"

The girls looked a little ashamed, muttering apologies, reprimanding each other for their lack of empathy.

"Besides," I said, "He has all three gems up there."

Even when children know they shouldn't do something, they really can't help themselves. They're curiosity is insatiable. When my youngest son was about 3, I was very into sewing and I had purchased a little magnet that was attached to the end of a telescopic rod. It was really very excellent for retrieving dropped pins without climbing under your desk and hunting for them. I had been a mother for quite a long time at this point and I knew nothing was sacred or safe in a house with small children. What's mine was theirs and what's theirs was theirs. And their sibling's things – also theirs. Basically, everything in the world belongs to small children. Still, despite this knowledge, I sat all the children down on the couch and I very seriously showed them the magnet. "Okay, guys. See this? It's mine. It's not a toy. It's not for play or for 'borrowing' or even for touching. In fact, don't even look at it."

The children chuckle nervously and some of them avert their eyes. Those are the obedient ones, they are my favourites that day. I continued to illustrate the rules about the magnet (don't touch it) and what we were never going to do (touch it). My talk was really very long and I think some of them began to doze.

"So," I say, "who does this belong to?"

The younger ones' cheer in answer, "Mummy!"

The older ones roll their eyes, they don't care about my magnet, they only care about their phones.

"That's right," I say, "And what are we not going to do?"

"Touch the magnet!" the younger ones' yell.

The older ones ask if they can go, they have friends to text.

I dismiss the children and feel secure that my magnet is safe. The next day it goes missing. I interrogate everyone in the house. I try to cut deals with some of the kids to rat out their siblings. But no one is talking. It's like Fight Club and they're all loyal to the first rule. They were all so adamant that none of them had taken it that I started to question my own sanity and whether *I* had lost the magnet. I'd lost a collective of about 4 years of my life in sleep at this point so it was possible. About a week later I'm stripping my son's bed to wash his sheets and there, under his pillow, is my magnet. Its telescopic rod is out and bent at an alarming angle, it has compound fractures in many places. And it is covered all over in band-aids. *So many band-aids*. I call my son in and hold the magnet out accusingly,

"Well?" I say.

He hangs his head, "Oh mama," he says, "I was just looking at your magnet. And it bwoke! I bandaged it and stuck it under my pillow and I checked it evewyday but it never got any better. I'm so vewy vewy sowwy."

And the thought of him all concerned, pulling out the magnet every day and checking on it made me laugh so hard that I couldn't even be mad.

You really can't have any nice things and simultaneously have small children. If you have anything you hold dear you may as well box it up and shove it in the top of your closet and wait until your children are at least 12 before you pull it out again. When I was pregnant with my eldest daughter my mother in law was telling a story about how she once found her hair dryer exactly as she left it but with the curly cord that attached it to the wall snipped neatly in two. A pair of scissors lay nearby. Many years had passed since that incident and she laughed as she told the story and said that it must have been one of her children but she wasn't sure who. My boyfriend looked sheepish and said, "I think that was me, actually."

"Was it really?" My mother in law asked, "I'd always wondered."

I looked at them as though they'd both each grown a second head, shocked at how calm they both were. I was sure that my own mother would have grounded me for life, even if I'd been 93 when I finally confessed.

"Why on earth did you cut it?" I asked.

My boyfriend shrugged, "I guess I just wanted to see if it would cut?"

This answer distressed me, "What do you *mean*, 'if it would cut'? They were scissors! What did you *think* would happen?"

But my mother in law said, "No, I understand. Sometimes you just get an urge to see what will happen if you do something."

At the time, I thought they were both bonkers but I do understand that now. It's like me poking the pipis or shoving that bead up my nose. The call of the void.

21st of July 2007 – The Journals

The baby rolled and swished for ages last night. I could have sat quietly for hours just soaking in the wonder of it. My morning sickness has slowed finally, leaving me feeling fantastic. Gosh, how delightful is the second trimester? Maybe it's just that the movements are more regular now but I've been feeling a lot more relaxed too. I started making a book for the kids called, "My Mummy is Having a Baby" to help them understand. The older children have a good grasp on it but A has never seen anyone pregnant or with a newborn so it's all new for him. Last time I tried to explain it to him I said, "Mummy has a baby in her tummy." He looked at me for a moment, as though weighing up the situation before beaming and cheerfully announcing, "I have a baby in my pants!"

Suffice to say, I don't think he understands.

SIBLINGS

At some point, you may have successfully repressed the pain of birth and the sleepless nights and decide you want to have a second child. You may feel a little apprehensive about this and fear that you won't be able to love this child as much as your firstborn, who you look at as though they hung the moon, even while they're picking their nose. I understand. I had the same fear when I was pregnant with my second and I took these fears to my mother in law who assured me that although your heart feels full to the brim already, it just somehow expands with each child and you love them all as much as each other. Which was very wise of her and also very true.

As I was an only child for the first 8 years of my life, my childhood and my brothers didn't have a lot of cross over and so we missed most of the joys and trials siblings closer in age may enjoy (or not, as the case may be). I was fascinated by siblings and the strange web of inside jokes that run between them. One time, while breakfasting with my cousins who were two years older and two years younger than me respectively, the eldest just looked at the youngest and they both just dissolved into giggles at nothing at all. Except of course, it was something. But this is the secret life of siblings. Your children, should you have more than one, will have a bond that is unique unto them. Biology seems to not be a factor in this as two of my friends are very close and each have a daughter, 5 years apart. They are 'soul sisters' who sleep at each other's houses and share meals and holidays and who I'm quite sure can dissolve into giggles at nothing just by looking at each other. Siblings will understand family ties and rules and will be able to tell each other accusingly, even years later, exactly who rolled who in a carpet and left them with claustrophobia for the rest of their lives.

For yourself you may have practical concerns about juggling the load of an additional child. When I was on a mothering forum years ago for women with large families, most people said they found going from one child to two children to be a fairly easy transition. Going from two to three seemed to be a bit of a juggle and then from four upwards, it went a bit easier. One woman said that when she told her brother she was expecting her sixth child and was worried about how she would cope that he said, "Ahh, don't worry, sis. It just means you will have to put another potato in the soup pot." I have clung to that sage advice on the most literal of levels and all of my children will attest that if I'm cooking a big soup or making mashed potatoes, and they ask how many to peel I will answer, "One for each person."

At some point, you will decide to tell your child that they are to be a 'big brother/sister'. When I was pregnant with my last baby, my son was so thrilled with the prospect of becoming a big brother that he came to me one morning, very solemn, and said, "When the baby is born I will love her so much. And if she ever gets prickles in her feet, I will pick them out." Which was probably the most heroic thing he could think of at 3-years-old. It's a hard concept for many children to grasp however and I've tried all sorts of tactics to explain the process of pregnancy and birth including making them a picture book with us as the starring characters and buying them *Where Did I Come From?* which in hindsight, is probably not aimed at 5 year olds. Nevertheless, they more or less get it except when I was pregnant with my first son, who had a nickname I later realised sounded remarkably like 'Santa'. My 3-year-old daughter came to me asking for a toy she had seen in a catalogue and I told her she would have to ask Santa Claus since it was so close to Christmas. She came over, bent close to my stomach and said, "Baby Santa, for Christmas I would like…" I found this hysterical and promptly went and drew a red Christmas hat on my ultrasound picture and stuck it on the fridge, which probably did little to alleviate the confusion.

Another time my Nanna called me to tell me about my cousin who had taken her 5-year-old to visit a friend who had just had a baby. My cousin introduced her daughter to the new little boy and said something like, "Remember when Shelly had a big stomach because the baby was in there? Look! Now he's out." On the way home, my cousin asked if her daughter had liked the baby and the little girl got quiet and then said, "Yes, I did. But why did Shelly swallow the baby in the first place?"

. . .

In the beginning, when juggling two children you will find that just when you thought you couldn't get any more tired, you do. If anyone suggests you sleep while the baby sleeps, forgetting that you have another child who will demolish the house like a small tornado, you may find you want to swallow them whole. Whenever you do need to sit to feed the baby, another of your children will emerge from the woodwork to request snacks or a drink and they will tell you emphatically they will perish unless they receive it this minute. In the early days, it is wise to prepare as though you are going on a road trip even though you aren't going anywhere at all. Keep a water bottle filled for the older child and small snacks prepared that can be easily opened with one hand. Literally pack them a lunchbox if you must and keep it in the fridge, lest your small child die of starvation in the 30 minutes it takes their sibling to feed. Have a selection of quiet tasks that can be completed while you are sitting by the older child either with your help or without, such as reading books or colouring ins. And if all that fails, be forever grateful you live in an age of smart devices and put on Peppa Pig on your phone.

As your children get older they will begin to interact with each other in a way that will either melt your heart or make you want to sell them as a set on Gumtree. I can pinpoint the exact day when my third daughter got a promotion from 'baby' and was initiated into games with the older two.

When the two older girls were 3 and 4 they were obsessed with all things girly and we had a pirate's booty worth of plastic jewellery. The girls kept it in a fluffy faux fur sack and it was carefully given out by the eldest. She got all the pink jewellery even though they both loved pink the most because she was the eldest and therefore the default boss. My third daughter was crawling at the time and as such the girls' bedroom, while little girl heaven, was also full of choking hazards such as barbie shoes and those little plastic rings and clip on earrings. We had erected a gate at their door and she would pull herself to standing on the opposite side of it, staring in wide eyed wonder as her sisters donned their weight in plastic jewellery and gems and generally danced around looking like little blonde fairies. One day, the gate hadn't been shut properly and I found her standing at the bed, looking proud as punch, her sister's having placed so many strings of plastic pearls around her neck it's a wonder she hadn't collapsed under the weight. The girls conceded to putting up the small jewellery that the little one might choke on and allowed her to partake in dress ups thereafter, although she always had to have the third best colour because she was the newest apprentice.

They played together nicely much of the time, although my second eldest had a dead pan sassy streak she would unleash at random moments, always to the shock of her polite and proper older sister. My grandparents bought and painted a small table and chair set for the girls one year as a gift and they would sit there for their meals. That morning they were having hot chocolates and toast and my eldest was delicately nibbling hers, before picking up her mug and tweaking her pinkie as though she were an 19th century aristocrat and says, very politely, to her sister, "May I say, your shirt is inside out."

And her sister, not missing a beat, replies rather haughtily for one wearing her garments incorrectly, "And may *I* say, that *you*…are an egghead."

That particular fight seems delightfully quaint when I think of the throw down screaming matches and stealth sabotage that would occur as the children got older. One time I had to have a very stern talking to about pulling out hair to my eldest daughter after her younger sister began to look a bit threadbare. Another time my third daughter snipped her brother's finger with tongs 'pretending to be Dr. Zoidberg' and gave him a permanent scar. And nothing prepared me for two boys who seemed to just roll from one end of the house to the other, in a perpetual wrestle match.

You do find that you have to divide yourself at times, one child will need you more than the others (and this will change from week to week, day to day or even hour to hour). You will mediate endless arguments to the point where you begin to think you could have a career as a marriage counsellor. Sometimes one child will emerge as the alpha child, bossing all the others and sometimes you will find there is a clash of the titans as two fierce personalities collide. For the most part, my children seem to like each other. Whenever there are parent teacher interviews my son's teachers say that he always says his sister is his best friend. It warms my heart. It very nearly makes up for the time he trapped her in the washing basket and sat on top of it.

Undated 2014 – The Journals

I used to say I didn't get along with women. Family was different, but I just couldn't seem to make women friends. I just never really felt like I fit in, it seemed like I was always being judged or I was too young, or too old or I liked to go to bed very early, or I was weird because I don't really like to drink wine. At school drop offs I would quietly slip into the classroom and try to make myself as small as possible. I was the most infuriatingly apologetic person, as though my mere presence was an inconvenience to the world in general. But as I got older I realised that it wasn't that I didn't get along with women. I just hadn't found the right women. The right women may still say I'm weird for not liking wine, but then they tell me they still love me anyway.

WHAT IT MEANS TO BE A MOTHER

I was sitting there with my grandmother once and she was talking about her kids and when my father and his sisters were small. My dad grew up on a cattle farm, first dairy and then beef. The farm was huge, sprawling acres set into the side of a small mountain, full of gullies and gentle rises and cow pats that my cousins and I would lie out into a hopscotch pattern for games. The farm smelled like grass and water and animals. I know it was a lot of work and my grandparents did most of it themselves. When my dad was little, my grandmother was busy running the farm with my grandad and she would dress the kids and send them to play but they kept coming back naked. She said sometimes she would find their clothes and sometimes she wouldn't.

"It got so bad," she said, "that I started to dress them backwards. Shirts, pinafores, all with the buttons done up at the back so they couldn't undo them and lose their clothes."

I laughed, "Really?"

"I did!" she exclaimed, "I had to, they kept losing their bloody clothes!"

And she smiled when she said it, even though I'm sure it

drove her mad at the time. She smiled like she was right there looking at those kids in that moment. Like it was the best time of her life, which I think is what motherhood really is. Even when it's awful, it's still the best time of your life.

I read once that if you want to know a woman you must first ask about her mother because that is where our story really begins. I found this interesting, both because family dynamics is fascinating to me and because I was startled by the truth of it. Of how our mothers really shape who we are, and how they contribute their brushstrokes to the portrait of ourselves as women and as mothers ourselves. If I had to describe my Mother I would say my mother is the kind of woman that gets things done. She doesn't really do emotions, she isn't much of a hugger. She is a woman who shows her love in a different way. She shows up. She showed up to cheer in football games despite freezing temperatures. She showed up at school graduations, parent teacher interviews and tennis matches and concerts. She did the school runs, the tae-kwon-do runs, the tennis runs, the football runs. She cooked meals after full days at work. She ferried us to mate's houses. She picked us up from parties. She showed up when I moved 200kms away and did the drive like it's no big deal, just to have cake on a birthday. She showed up when I called her stranded halfway to Brisbane and was so sick I couldn't move let alone make the rest of the trip. She answers the phone when you call her at 5am to say you've given birth. She answers the phone when you call her at 3am to say your house burnt down. She calls you when she gets off a plane because she knew you needed her but she didn't know why. She says all the right things that make all the sadness and anger you felt over a situation fall away because you poured your troubles into her hands and she took them from you. She shows up when you needed her. She keeps your secrets and your confidences and never tells a soul. My mother shows up. I like to think that I am like her, but the truth is that I always feel like I fall short in some respect. But sometimes, when I feel like I'm really dropping the ball, when I arrive at school in the middle of the morning, harried, with my hair askew bearing a platter of store bought cookies for the Christmas party I forgot about until the second the child was getting out of the car – at least I showed up. I might be shy to stand up and sing during school Christmas carol concerts, I might be five minutes late with a baby on my hip, I might be putting birthday candles into a Woolies mudcake, but you know what? I showed up.

I think most of us feel like we are fumbling through, like we drop too many balls and no one catalogues their failures better than a mother. Sometimes it starts early, pregnancy or birth. After my fifth son was born, when he was 19 days old, I just cried and cried because I had this vision of how I expected his homebirth to be and I felt like I had let myself down by not achieving it. It was unfounded of course, his birth was almost textbook in its progression but I had imagined me standing on our wide verandah, rocking my hips while I looked at the cows grazing in the field and instead I was ashamed of the way I had cried towards the end in frustration and pain and how at the mercy of my body I had become. I thought I had been weak. My midwife came by for a check-up and I remember asking her what was wrong with me that I had been so horrible during birth. And she looked stunned and said, "Why on earth would you think that?"

. . .

I could probably give you a long list off the top of my head of the ways I felt I failed as a mother. And I know that I'm not alone and that women are the hardest on themselves. We try to be everything to everyone and berate ourselves for the slightest thing. Library books we forgot, the free dress day we missed, the laundry we had to wash twice because we didn't take it out of the machine when it finished. We bully ourselves for not eating properly, or not working out enough, or for having perfectly normal cellulite. We worry we don't make enough money, we don't contribute enough to society, we don't stand up in the eyes of our peers – even those of us who excel. We feel bad when our kids ask for a new toy and we can't afford it, even while we know they don't need it because they have a hundred toys and don't play with half of them. We feel bad when their shoelace breaks as though we got up in the middle of the night and cut it half way through in a sabotage mission.

For me this sometimes compounds at special occasions. At Christmas time, my stress levels seem to escalate until I find myself having to deep breathe in Kmart before I scream. I've come to realise that I live my life in a state of perpetual stress and I'm never really 'on the ball' but more rushing from fire to fire trying to put out the one that is most likely to reduce the house to cinders at any given moment. I have lists everywhere, groceries, school break up events, extracurricular activity events, present lists, food lists, family event lists, and whose idea was it to make the children's six monthly dental check-ups coincide with the end of the school year anyway? But the mental lists? They overwhelm me. I turn from a normalish mum who mostly just loses her mind on a bi-weekly basis into a raving woman with dishevelled hair, melting down in the supermarket because there were only full-sized candy canes and I need mini candy canes for Christmas cards, goddammit. Of course, I'm not really distressed about the actual candy canes, I'm distressed that I have too many things on my mental list and this one hasn't been as simple as I hoped.

At any given time, a mother may have a mental list, mental calendar, mental alarm clock etc., in her head. She's reminding herself it's bin day, that she needs to find a library book, that Timmy has outgrown his shoes, that she needs to pick up broccoli and apples and milk from the store, that she needs to book Ruby in to the hairdressers, that she hasn't eaten yet today…and that is before we throw in a job and then she's also trying to find time to show up to the office without cereal in her hair. I know a lot of women married to a man who will say their husband is helpful. I am not discounting that. *(Although a little part of me starts screaming, you shouldn't be 'helpful', you should do half the damn work because that's what partnership is, for god's sake!)* However, the statistical reality is, in Australia today the lion's share of domestic duties still falls on women. Women are expected to keep house, raise babies, work the 9-5 and do it all while feeding everyone all organic fruits harvested by fair trade fairies and look like they're an Instagram influencer while doing it. And fuck that noise. The physical load of those tasks is too much for any one person and it is *nothing* compared to the mental load of that weighing on you. It's why when someone says, "Tell me if you need help," you will find women don't, even if they desperately *need* help. The act of seeking help, mentally cataloguing the tasks into what you must do yourself and what another person can do, delegating those tasks, explaining how those tasks need to be done, it's too much. It might be taking away one of your physical tasks

– maybe – but it's adding another 3-4 things to your mental load, and it's too much to deal with.

The saying goes that it takes a village to raise a child. Now days it seems that most women not only do not have a village, they barely have a support network at all. Our pre-natal support is minimal and amounts to having your urine and blood pressure checked at varying intervals, often not even by the same health care team, our birth support amounts to one or two overworked midwives who, bless them, often do not get the credit they deserve for guiding two people safely through one of the most critical times of their lives. Postnatally you receive around 24-48 hours in hospital, sometimes less for subsequent mothers – despite the fact that many women haven't adequately gotten the hang of breastfeeding yet, should they choose to do so. There is little to no community support for new mothers once they come home with a small person they are entrusted to care for 24 hours a day on little sleep, all while they're recovering from a physical event that was incredibly taxing on their body, never mind our mothers who have had major abdominal surgery to birth their children. Remarkably, despite postnatal depression rates, women rally to the challenge. We succeed, however much we feel like we are drowning under the weight of our responsibilities, in managing all the hundreds of things we must do each week to ensure well-adjusted children. We are not robots, or computers, or perfect beings, but humans with flaws and faults and needs, who sometimes – purely because our physical and mental loads are so heavy – drop a ball. Motherhood demands selflessness.

I read a post on my Facebook Memories the other day from the week before summer holidays ended and I was fretting. I had contacted over 50 books, labelled pencils, named hats. I had spent three days baking school snacks and organising lunchboxes and cleaning the house top to bottom so everything would be in order before the kids went back to school.

One of my friends wrote, "You're way more organised than I am. What are you worried about?"

And I responded, "I guess I'm just scared I'm forgetting something. Like I'm going to drop a ball somewhere."

And she said, "You know what? Balls bounce."

Balls bounce. The hardest part about being a mother isn't the sleepless nights, it isn't childbirth or school projects. It's forgiving yourself for not being perfect and then realising you never needed forgiveness in the first place. Because balls bounce.

Porcupine Meatballs – The Recipe Book

Ingredients:
1kg of minced beef
1 onion grated
2 eggs
¼ of a cup of Plain Flour
½ cup of cooked rice
2 tins of condensed tomato soup
Water

Optional:
Grated carrot, grated zucchini or any other vegetables you wish to attempt to hide.

Method:

1. *Open tins of condensed tomato soup and pour into a large saucepan, keeping one empty can aside.*
2. *Fill empty can with water X4 and add to pot, stir well and put on to boil.*
3. *Cook your rice, rinse, drain and set aside.*
4. *Place minced beef in a bowl and mix in eggs.*
5. *Mix in onion and any other vegetables.*
6. *Mix in flour.*
7. *Put rice into the mixture and mix well using hands.*
8. *Begin rolling meatballs, slightly smaller than a golf ball size and place these into your tomato soup mixture.*
9. *Turn heat down to a simmer and cook for 40 minutes, gently flipping meatballs occasionally during.*
10. *Serve with mashed potato and your choice of steamed vegetables.*

FEEDING THE TRIBE

I'm going to just straight up say this. Your kids are almost definitely going to hate basically everything you put in front of them. Nothing fills me with more despair about the state of my life than meal planning for the upcoming week or cooking dinners. The sun begins to go down and I feel this dread descend on me as I realise it's nearly time to make dinner again and I feel like screaming, "Argh! I literally just fed you yesterday!" While I was trying to figure out a title for this memoir I nearly called it "7846 dinners" because I got on a website that calculated how many days you've been alive based on your birthday and entered my eldest daughters date of birth into it. Honestly, it's a real ordeal. If you are a mother that loves to cook, more power to you and please come live with me. For me though, it's always been an exercise in juggling nutrients in with tantrums out. From almost the moment I first give them a taste of solids as babies they screw up their little faces at me in disgust and this just continues until they leave home, I think.

This is how every evening goes at my house. There is me,

standing in the kitchen, cooking dinner and remembering with longing the days my mother would cook for me and thinking about how the Brady Bunch had six kids and they had an Alice and I have six kids but no Alice, how is that fair? I want an Alice. In the middle of all this one kid will bounce into the kitchen and say with great enthusiasm, "What's for dinner?" I really admire this about my kids. Despite the fact that I've disappointed at least one of them for 2 decades worth of dinners, they still manage to be optimistic every night. I will usually try to deflect this question to delay the inevitable tantrum but eventually I will say something like, "Tacos."

One kid will cheer from the lounge room.

One kid will groan loudly and announce that Tacos smell like a kid at her school with bad BO and she can't possibly eat Tacos ever again, because she hates them and didn't we *just* have them?

And then replace Tacos with literally any other dinner choice and just go ahead and have the conversation again on a different day with a different collaboration of children. *Seven Thousand, Eight Hundred and Forty-Freaking-Six times.*

There is only one thing that my kids all eat. Porcupine Meatballs. I am also partial to them because I can hide finely grated veggies in them and they don't usually notice but even if they do they still eat them but just say, "Please, please, Mummy, don't put any of that orange stuff in mine next time."

"Carrots? But you like carrots! You made me cut some up for your school lunch."

"I only like raw carrots now. I don't like the cooked ones anymore."

I'm a firm believer that you need to find something you can hide vegetables in, like a reverse poisoner who just wants people to be healthy. Some people have even dedicated entire books or blogs to the hiding of foods in other foods, like magicians. One of my friends makes a chocolate slice with zucchini hidden in it. Hiding a vegetable in a sweet? Girl, you are next level stealthy. The legend walks amongst us.

One time, when she was about five, my middle daughter started hiding her dinners. It was a really rough time for me because I was pregnant with my youngest son and so sick, constantly vomiting so I would dish up dinner and retreat somewhere away from the smells with my dry toast or something equally bland. This meant that I could hear but not see the dinnertime being had by the kids and whenever she didn't like something, my daughter would just hide her food somewhere when her sisters weren't looking, or wait until they finished and got up from the table and announce she was done. Usually her hiding spots were fairly unimaginative like, the bin, for example. Or she might feed little bits to the dog, or she would just put it in the fridge. So, I got in the habit of checking her plate when she announced she was done and trying to make sure there wasn't any food in the bin or the fridge or that the dog didn't look particularly plump that evening. One night, it all came undone though because I had just dished up spaghetti bolognese, left the room to vomit over the smells and she met me at the bathroom door, not 5 minutes later with a completely empty plate and said she had eaten it all.

"No way," I said.

"I did!" she announced proudly.

I squinted my eyes at her and immediately went to check the bin. Nothing. Fridge? Nothing. I eyed the dog who absolutely could not have eaten the entire serving in that time frame. I questioned the other kids, who had been embroiled in a deep discussion about Lizzie McGuire and couldn't remember anything except she left the room with her plate. I just couldn't find this missing dinner anywhere. I started to look in really random places like the clothes hamper and the kids' drawers but kept coming up empty.

"Where is it?" I kept asking.

"I ate it," she insisted. I felt like I was on an episode of NCIS. Then her eyes darted to the coffee table. It was this weird piece of furniture, a squat teak wooden table we had picked up from a boutique store in Brisbane that had cupboards on each side of it, and drawers in the middle and it sat barely two inches off the ground. I open the cupboards and found them empty. Very reluctantly I open each of the six drawers, already imagining trying to clean up juicy spaghetti bolognese from the crevasses of the drawers, god, I would never get the smell out, it would seep into the wood. My stomach was rolling at the thought. The drawers were empty. My child beams at me and I am starting to really think I am losing it because she can't, she *cannot*, have finished the entire plate in 5 minutes, but I just can't find this dinner anywhere so I send her off to play and we finish up the night and the kids are brushing their teeth when suddenly I sit up like I've just been bitten. I go to the coffee table and it's really very heavy but I push it to the side and there, on the cream carpet is a pile of upended spaghetti bolognese. The juices have all seeped into the carpet. The girls are all standing there looking at me, stunned, and the two older ones were clutching at each other in mortification.

"*Why* would you put your dinner on the *carpet*?"

"Well," she says, "you kept checking the bin."

We have ended up compromising in that each child is allowed to choose just *one* dish that they can absolutely refuse to eat. So, for my second eldest daughter this is tuna mornay. She hates it, it makes her gag. That's it for her, her get out of dinner free card. You have to be very careful with this though as one night my son announced his one dinner would be chicken soup. He hated it and he would eat absolutely anything except chicken soup. Then the next night when lasagne was served for dinner he said he changed his mind and he wanted lasagne to be his one dinner. I think he would have kept going every night if he could have gotten away with it. One dinner only which can be changed once a year only, those are the rules. These are just the rules for us as none of my kids have any food intolerances or allergies and we aren't dealing with any serious food aversions that is a whole new ballgame entirely and those mothers deserve an awards night because I have witnessed the frustration and tears with some of my friends and it's no joke. My children are just run of the mill fussy eaters. A few times I have been told that the reason my kids are so fussy is because I'm a giant marshmallow of a mother who doesn't do stuff like serve them the previous night's dinner for breakfast but I think it's genetic because I'm really fussy with food myself. I always order the same thing no matter where I go. I will look at the menu as though I'm studying it but I already know I'm damn well going to order the chicken caesar salad.

Another thing we do in my house is something I call, 'Whatever Night'. The kids all cheer when I announce Whatever Night. It's basically me saying they are fending for themselves and whatever they can find, that's what they can eat. They race to the fridge and freezer and pull out frozen pizza or start cooking up eggs and bacon and they delight in it. It's perfect for those nights that you just cannot deal with another dinner but you have too much stuff in the house to justify takeaway.

Or you just can't bear the thought of getting in the car to get the takeaway. The downside is that Whatever Night really only works when you have kids who are old enough to fend for themselves, otherwise it's just you making different dinners for everyone like they're at a restaurant. I've heard of some families having their own household versions of the Can't Be Stuffed dinner including, Cheap Tuesday where they eat the frozen leftovers or do toasties or Breakfast for Dinner where they just serve up cereal. I think you really have to have some kind of back-up plan for the nights where you woke up late and one kid forgot their lunchbox and your boss was being unreasonable and you got stuck in traffic and you just can't cope with the thought of dinner. It doesn't make you lazy. It makes you prepared for a domestic apocalypse. Because 7846 dinners? That's crazy.

OFF TO SCHOOL

My daughter's boyfriend's mother seems like the mythical perfect mother to me. She is on the P&C and works the tuckshop and sometimes she goes to school events even when her own children aren't participating. On the other hand, I feel like when I turn up to school I'm always harried, wearing a hippie skirt and with crumbs on my shirt and wild, wavy hair that sometimes resembles Hagrid on a bad hair day. I always feel like everyone is looking at me wondering if I even own a hairbrush or a mirror and whether I'm actually a mother or if they should call the school office and inform them that a homeless woman is loitering outside school grounds. The answer is that they probably are not thinking that or even noticing me at all. Everyone thinks people are always looking at them but they usually aren't because most people have enough problems of their own without adding your shirt crumbs on top. I've lost count of the amount of times I've had to ask my daughter to ask her boyfriend to ask his mother if it's free dress day tomorrow or if I've missed the deadline for the school excursion payment and every time I do I feel like I'm back in school asking to borrow someone's homework so I can copy the answers. Just the other day one of my kids asked if it was a pupil free day on Monday and I was like, "Oh, that's a Brooke question. That's not a question for me. You're going to have to ask your other mother." Because I like to pretend we are co-parenting the children since I'm constantly having to ask if I can copy her homework. I wasn't always so clueless, I use to read the newsletters and carefully write the dates in my diary but I just can't seem to manage it anymore, so if you are also like me the best thing I can suggest is you find yourself a school wife. Your school wife is the one who will remind you about events and payments and you will feel like you have someone who has your back. I don't think Brooke has a school wife. She has it together. She goes to P&C meetings and fights for uniform change. I have to battle enough at home for the kids to have matching socks. It's a problem. One time my son tried to get out of the car with one long white sock and one tiny black one with a lacy frill along the top which belonged to his sister. Trust me, I'm fighting a different war.

Once upon a time though, several children ago, I did have my finger on the pulse when it came to schooling. Before my eldest was even ready to go to school I tried to teach her to read. I made flashcards with the alphabet, I wrote signs for everything in the house and tacked them on to the items to try and teach her their written names by her seeing them all the time and I would sit with her and we would go over readers every day. She did not learn to read. She simply wasn't ready. It seemed really important that she know how to read early though so I persisted even though she was towards the end of grade 1 before it finally clicked. It seemed really important that her hair was done in elaborate styles before school each day with ribbons to match the uniform and that her pencils were labelled with stickers and not just permanent marker. It seemed so incredibly important she win the colouring in competition at Easter that I asked the school about 5 times in a week when it would be judged and then I nearly framed the first place certificate. I'm surprised I don't make her include it with her resume now when she applies for jobs. I would write letters of complaint about the homework or the excursions. I stopped writing letters of complaint after my daughter broke her tooth.

When my daughter was in grade 1 they began the 'Munch and Crunch' initiative. My kids still have this now only it's just called 'Fruit Break'. Now it is mostly about giving the kids a little burst of energy by stopping for a fruit break before they have Morning Tea but when my eldest was younger it was also supposed to be about helping them learn to talk properly by exercising their jaws with hard fruit and vegetables. We received a letter home with acceptable fruit and vegetables (apples, carrots, pears etc) and unacceptable fruits and vegetables (bananas, watermelon etc). Basically, soft fruits were bad and hard fruits were good. I had two issues with this, the first being that I was very frugal and bananas cost $0.99 for a kg but apples cost $4.99 per kg and the second was that my daughter had a very wobbly bottom tooth and it hurt her to eat hard foods. I wrote a...very stern letter. I was embarrassingly vocal about this issue. It was a whole deal. I used my best handwriting. I may have underlined some words. That afternoon I got a response that was short in it's response and basically amounted to, "Of course she can eat a banana, relax, nutjob."

. . .

A couple of days after this I got a call from the school saying that my daughter was at the sick bay as she had broken her tooth while eating lunch and could I come and get her. I raced down there and immediately took her to the dentist for an emergency appointment. One of her bottom baby teeth had snapped in half and the dentist said it looked like she had gotten a fracture in it at some point, which had weakened over time and snapped. Since it was a little wobbly anyway, they just pulled it out in the chair and we took it home for the tooth fairy. When she got back in the car I asked her what had happened. She told me she had been eating morning tea and ate one of the homemade cookies I had baked her and it had just snapped right off. I feel the need to tell you here there was *nothing wrong with my cookies*. I assure you they are actually gooey, soft, heavenly little discs of deliciousness but, yes, it was my cookie that broke the tooth. I know I sound defensive. Whatever. The next day I dropped her in to school and the teacher said, "How is her tooth?"

And I said, "Oh yes, good. It was wobbly anyway so they just pulled it out."

And she smiled sweetly and said, "Well. Thank goodness it wasn't an apple, hey?"

Karma. She will really spank you hard sometimes.

I think the hardest part about having school kids is the homework. The juggle in itself is hard, the last thing anyone feels like doing at the end of the day is more work. Sometimes I can barely make it through the 10-minute drive home without losing it. I will be sitting there watching them walk up to the car and they look so sweet and my son is carrying his little sister's bag for her and I'll think, "Wow. They're so perfect."

Then they get in the car and my teenage daughter will say, "Okay, you really need to speak to your son because…"

Before I'm even out of the carpark I'm wondering if it's okay to shot whiskey at 3:30 in the afternoon. The kids are hot and exhausted and sweaty and someone definitely didn't put on deodorant that morning and when we get home we all just want to get as far away from each other as possible. But there is homework.

Here is the other problem with homework. I can't do maths. I really can't. My brain just shuts down. I can almost see it go on screensaver mode and I know I *could* figure it out but I just can't, absolutely *cannot* do it, because it's so boring. And because I can't make my brain function to do maths I also have no idea how to perform maths beyond a fifth grade level. I've repressed all of high school maths and I don't even feel bad about it. I do have a friend who has a PhD in maths though, so occasionally I have been known to send her a message and beg and plead that she help my child in maths. I have no idea how I will ever repay her unless her daughter one day decides she needs to learn how to use a spinning wheel and then I have her back. Homework kind of feels like parental punishment. The kids don't want to do it, you don't want to do it, didn't you suffer enough having to do your own homework? From speaking to friends who are teachers, even they hate homework. Despite this reluctance on absolutely everyone's behalf, we persist in sitting at the table, painstakingly doing our readers and maths until you have to stop so you don't ruin your family bonds forever. I've tried to put a silver lining on most things I've written, but I've got nothing here. Death to homework. The end.

School lunches, school assemblies, school projects, free dress days, book week, Easter bonnet parades, end of year concerts, school discos…these are the years it all happens. The upside is you suddenly have 6 free hours a day but many mothers spend those working either in the home or out so it isn't quite the respite you hoped it would be. School is a huge part of your parenting journey, including kinder and the states that have prep it's going to be 12-14 years of your child's life. Some of you will have children that take to academia like ducks to water and some kid's it simply doesn't mesh with, especially kids who learn outside the norm. Some of my children have been wonderful students who get good grades and others have really had to struggle. The interesting thing is, even the kids who do struggle usually have one subject they just kick ass in. It might not even be a school subject, just an aspect of one. One of my daughters consistently failed English right up until tenth grade but she is excellent at Film and TV. She and her project partner made this amazing short thriller film that was so good that when we showed it to the younger kids I had trouble getting them to go to sleep because they were frightened. I was like, "But you know that was just Lachlan. You *know* him. You saw him today. He's *fine*." One of my other kids struggles a lot but knows everything there is to know about dinosaurs and one year he secretly went to violin lessons and didn't tell anyone because he wanted it to be a surprise but forgot to tell me before the concert so I didn't show up and then he came out after school and said, "Why didn't you come to my violin concert?"

And I was like, "You…you do violin?"

Luckily my friend had a daughter that went too and she had a video of it.

Academia is important but it's also important to make sure that your kids know that everyone has different strengths and they are so much more than a NAPLAN score or an A in Science. School is a huge part of their life but a little part of who they are. You can be there to help them and guide them and work with them but it's so important that your children don't believe their value only lies in how well they do in their schooling. Not everyone is going to tread the same path and sometimes it's the kids that have to make their own way that end up doing some really wonderful things. I often think it is cruel that we insist children decide what they want to be when they're so young. By mid high school they are forced to choose subjects for the higher grades and those subjects determine what they might study at university, which in turn decides what career they will have. How would anyone know what they want to do at 14? Once my mother said to me when she was in her 40's, "Even *I* don't know what I want to be when I grow up."

Schooling can be a real ordeal. Almost every mother I know lives for the school holidays and counts down and cannot wait for the end of term. And almost every mother I know is ready to get down on her two knees and thank the lord school holidays are over by the end of them. Both feelings are completely valid.

The funny thing is, almost all the things I complain about from birth through to teenagers are the parts of parenting I secretly don't mind so much. Like the fact my five-year-old will come and ask me something and use a word that isn't correct or say a sentence that doesn't make sense, and when I say I don't understand she will repeat the *exact same word* just slower or louder like she is speaking to someone of incredibly low intelligence.

"What day is tomorrow?"
"Friday."
"No. What *day* is tomorrow?"
"Tomorrow is Friday."
"No. The day after today. *What day* is it?"
"Dude. It's Friday. I don't know what answer you want."
"The day after today."
"Tomorrow?"
"Yes. What *day* is that?"
"Tomorrow is Friday."
"No. WHAT…DAY…IS…IT?"
"….you need to go play."

It's infuriating. It makes me want to stab myself to death with a spoon. But it's absolutely hilarious and that's what I love about parenting. Maybe it's because I've been on this carousel for almost two decades now. But all those things that drive you insane today? They're so funny in 10 years time. One day your house will be clean, your car won't have smashed milk arrowroot on the carpet, your kids will hold conversations that actually make sense and you will *miss* this insanity.

Let me tell you a story about when my daughter was at school. It's one of my favourites. To set the scene my eldest daughter is seven years old. You wouldn't know it to look at her now but she had this incredible temper when she was little. Unless they experienced one of her infrequent but volatile rages, most people didn't believe me. This particular day it is summer and I am taking the kids to school. My Nanna took us because I didn't drive back then and I was about 25 weeks pregnant with my first son and fourth child. Nanna was waiting in the car with my youngest daughter who was three years old and was going to go to swimming lessons with her auntie that day. I am walking my seven-year-old and six-year-old daughters into their catholic school. Both girls are feeling quite happy and chattering and everything was going fine. I was carrying really big with my son and I was feeling ungainly, with girls I have a teeny compact rock melon under my dress, with boys…well one time when I was pregnant with my youngest son I posted a photo of my belly at 15 weeks pregnant on a mothering forum and one of my friends mentioned that in another group they were discussing how I couldn't *possibly* be that big and it must be a photo from a *previous* pregnancy. It wasn't.

I'm waddling the girls into school and I mention to the six-year-old that it is water play at her class today. She had swimmers and a towel and her class was going to play with sprinklers and buckets of water and have a grand old time.

The eldest says, "Why does she get water play and I don't?"

I explain that her class is just having a water play day, I don't know, I don't make the rules. She immediately launched into how unfair this was. One sister is getting water play and one is getting to go swimming and she was getting *nothing*.

"I can take you swimming at Nanna's after school," I offered, even though squeezing myself into a swimsuit seemed like some form of torture.

This was not good enough. She begins saying that this is also unfair because then her sisters have done two water things and she has only done one. I can tell things are getting serious by this point and I'm desperately trying to defuse the bomb, but there is nothing I can offer her because I can't very well have her sisters sit outside the pool on the grass like poor little orphans while I take her swimming because she feels hard done by. My eldest daughter's friends spot her and wave hello. She glares at them. Then she explodes.

"I DON'T WANT TO GO TO SCHOOL! I DON'T WANT TO GO TO SCHOOL!"

Most of my kids behave really well in public and save their moments of fury and rage for me alone because they have the good sense to be embarrassed about throwing a tantrum in public but on this day, she had no such concerns. I kiss the youngest goodbye and push her towards her classroom and away from her sister's wrath. People are really beginning to stare by this point. I'm trying to squat down to calm this child while also trying to not fall over because my centre of gravity has been displaced. The bell rings and it was assembly day so kids begin to move towards the hall. Throngs of beautifully well-behaved children and me clutching my demon child's hand while she struggles to free herself all the while screaming at the top of her lungs, "I DON'T WANT TO GO TO SCHOOL!"

At the doorway to the hall the Principal comes up to us and tries to talk my daughter into coming inside and – I kid you not – she *hisses* at him. Then screams in his face. He retreats. I don't blame him. At this point, basically every head in the school is turned towards my daughter wailing. People whisper to my younger daughter who is sitting placidly with her class. Privately she looks pleased because she will forever be known as the 'good sister' and also because she will have mad street cred for living with such a crazy person and surviving.

. . .

I begin to realise I cannot take her in. This temper tantrum will run its own course but she absolutely cannot go to school today. So, I turn to my screaming child and I say, "Okay. We are going home."

But I do it in that mum way. You know the way. Your voice is calm but your eyes reflect the fires of hell and the kid knows things just got real and they're going to be in massive trouble. I can see the little cogs turning in her head as she realises all the lost television time about to come her way and she looks at me and starts screaming, "No! I WANT TO GO TO SCHOOL!"

She's hysterical. I half drag her towards the exit. She's screaming the whole way, "LET ME GO TO SCHOOL! LET ME GO TO SCHOOL!"

But I can't back down because I made a call and kids can smell weakness. It seems really strange to be pulling a child out of the school ground while they are screaming that they want to go to school. Any second I'm waiting for someone to make a citizen's arrest for kidnapping. She is digging her heels in and I'm trying to pull her along without damaging her arm socket, and it becomes clear the only way I'm getting her back to the car is if I carry her. So, I heft up this seven year old on my pregnant belly, while she is kicking and screaming and yelling, "LET ME GO TO SCHOOL!"

I am headed towards this little path behind the church and there are colourful flower beds. I see the parish priest walking a visitor around them, both marvelling at the roses while I am heading towards them with a kid that looks like she needs an exorcism. They're both wearing straw sunhats and pressed trousers and any second now I expect one of them to suggest they have some iced tea. Meanwhile, my hair has flung loose of my hair tie and I'm trying to keep my skirt up while I wrangle a child over half my size and who is thrashing like a fish on land. Just before we get to the priest and companion, my daughter does this wild whole-body buck and because my centre of gravity is off, I can't hold her or myself upright and it sends both of us sprawling on the concrete at the foot of the priest, my shoe breaks, my skirt rides up and I skin a knee. I burst into tears.

There we are. Both of us crying, me bleeding, one shoe and the priest looking on in horror. My little girl sniffles and looks at me and says, "Please mummy. I don't want to hurt you...but I will."

The priest recoils and retreats to the safety of his rose bushes.

Five minutes later I am hobbling back to the car, broken shoe in hand, both of us are still crying and Nanna jumps out and says, "What happened?!"

Where do I even begin?

Now, as far as shitty parenting days go, that was right up there. It was so far up there. It's one of my Top 5 Shitty Parenting Moments. But now we laugh about it. So, I guess it's also one of my Top 5 Most Hilarious Parenting Moments. What I'm trying to say is the real shitty stuff is the stuff you will never laugh about. Sickness, broken hearts, those heart stopping moments when you think 'There but for the grace of God, go I'. You've probably all had one of those. The day to day with kids is hard work, I'm not devaluing that, but it's fleeting. It really is. And it's so damn good as well. The hard stuff is part of the tapestry of your parenting journey. It just wouldn't be the same without it.

. . .

So, yes. You are going to cry and have some really hard days, but try to think, "Will I laugh about this one day?" "Will I miss this when she is 18 and walking out the door on a date?" For me the answer is almost always, yes.

Except for homework. It can get in the bin.

ON HAVING IT TOGETHER

The other day I called my Nanna to ask what age she was at when she really felt like she had it together and she laughed so hard that I thought I had a potential career in stand-up comedy.

"Oh, god, no," She said, "I don't think anyone has it together. Things just happen."

"Some people seem like they have it together though," I said, feeling alarmed because I really wanted her to say something like, 'oh yes, 40, everything just fell into place then', so I could just write the date on the calendar and wait for me to be able to get myself together.

"Those people don't have it together either," She said, "They just don't talk about it."

The thing is, not one month before this conversation I really did feel like I had it together. I was managing two jobs, my house was clean, *company* clean and the washing was all folded and put away. I had meal plans and I'd written lists so when the children got home from school they knew what time to start the dinner and every weekend I spent two hours cleaning the floors and bathrooms and watering the plants and I was feeling shocked and secretly smug thinking, "Dude. You have done it. Adulthood, I have arrived in all my magnificent glory."

Less than three weeks later I had resigned from my job because every single cell in my body was screaming at me, and I didn't have a plan and my other job isn't financially sustainable long term so I didn't know what came next but I knew I needed to leave. *Leave right now.* I hustled to find as much editing work as I possibly could and then I got the flu and genuinely thought I might die and then the kids finished school and they went off to their dad's leaving me and my second eldest at home.

If there is one thing I know categorically it's that she and I are totally useless adults when we don't have children to motivate us. Neither of us have any idea what small families eat. Seriously, no idea. The first night we had duck pancakes and then for the remainder of the week we ate like college frat boys and I began to be concerned that when the children leave home I would die of scurvy. I ran out of clean underwear and neither of us could find the motivation to run a load of washing because who can be bothered putting on a half a load? I was walking around in lacy underwear, the kind that go with lingerie because that was all I had left and I felt like I was getting ready to go on a date except I hadn't shaved my legs and my jeans were 3 days old. Around day five, I was sitting there thinking about how hard being an adult was and it reminded me of the time that my friend and I were doing a casual stalk of the Facebook page of a guy she met at a party and he wrote, "Existence should be consensual" and now every time I'm having a moment I think about that. I want it on a t-shirt. And I said to myself, "Girl, you really, really, *really* do *not* have it together."

In the middle of all this my beautiful friend sent me a message and asked me how I was because I must have psychically sent out an SOS. I'm sure she regretted that because I said, "I'm fine but I'm also a total wreck." And then I laid out all my troubles ranging from things that happened when I was 10 years old all the way up to present day and I told her my Nanna didn't think we *ever* get it together and goddamn it, all I want in life is to have my shit together. My friend was like, "That's a lot of stuff." But then she said that this was why we need a village because if we have a village then collectively we all can add something to the table and *together*, we have it together.

After speaking with my Nanna and my friend, I decided to write a list of what would make me feel like I had my life in order, because my teenage daughter and her boyfriend and I decided that even if you didn't have your life together, if you wrote a list of how you were going to get it together, you were halfway there. This is where I was at, I was seeking advice from anyone in an age bracket from 78 to 17, because I was in such despair I would take pearls of wisdom from wherever I could get them.

The list is really small. It's actually just 3 things. I decided that for me, the three things that would make me feel like I had my life together were:

1. Financial stability.
2. Healthy relationships (with a partner, or friends/family and definitely with yourself).
3. A safe, stable home.

Now these might not be the same for you. Or maybe you already have all three but the thing that would really make you feel like you had your life together is something like, better teeth. I don't know. Everyone is different. But for me, these were the three things. I don't think you necessarily get to have everything on your list all at the same time, or you will get to have them all but then you'll decide to leave your second job without a plan and suddenly you don't have one of them. Because, as Nanna said, things just happen. It was quite a liberating experience because I noticed I hadn't written on there, clean non-lacy underwear or trips to Hawaii or become Prime Minister. I do know this, staying in the second job might have helped me tick off number 1 on that list, but I wouldn't have had the second point on the list. So maybe I didn't have everything but as Meatloaf says, "Two outta three ain't bad."

So, I'm very sorry to say, you probably won't ever feel like you have it all figured out. Sometimes you will be really rocking it though and you should soak those times up, and wear your GirlWonder cape with pride. Then you'll realise that you made your salad sandwich for work but forgot the bread. This actually happened to me. Usually though, you will find you have *something* together. So maybe your shirt is inside out but you made a really excellent dinner last night. Or maybe you can't cook worth a damn but you read the bedtime story with all the voices. And if ever you are feeling very overwhelmed by things write down your list of what would make you feel like you have it together. You might surprise yourself and find you are closer than you think.

TWEENS

When my older girls turned eight I commissioned a woman to make wall quilts for them with photos printed on to fabric and in the centre, she handstitched a little outfit they had when they were a baby. I did this because, for me, eight years old always signified the end of the 'baby years' and the beginning of your life as a big kid. Baby teeth fell out and their legs grew long and coltish, they began to listen to and acquire a taste for music, they would develop a style for clothing and they no longer crawled into my lap to tell me a story. It was a time when 'Mummy' slowly became 'Mum' and when they read their books became thicker and the pictures disappeared from the pages. About a year ago, my youngest came to me and said, "Mama? My friends don't like that I still call you Mummy. They think it's babyish."

"Oh," I said, "Well, that's very mean of them. You can call me whatever you want to."

Except privately I was imagining me bailing up these little second grade punks and being all, "Listen up, you little snots. This is my last baby and if you ruin this for me, I will destroy you." I just wish I could put her on pause. Yet, here we are a year later and she still calls me Mummy but I've noticed that when she is speaking to other people she refers to me as Mum. Time stops for no mother.

When I was saving space for this chapter for the longest time it just said, "Ahh, my old nemesis" before I finally got around to writing the chapter. I believe that every parent has an age they find the most challenging, for some people that is the newborn stage, for other's it is the teenage years but for me, it's always been the ages eight to twelve. I don't even think I liked *me* at those ages. I think it's that you still have a lot of the trying parts of them being little, they will still cry at the drop of a hat but you also have the attitude of teenagers.

Recently while out to lunch with a friend I said that I think if I had waited to have children until I was older, I probably would have decided to remain childless. She laughed at me, as she knows I love babies and would have a hundred if I had the money, the years and if my body hadn't thrown up its hands in exasperation during my sixth child's pregnancy.

"Of course, I love *my* children," I said, "It's just that I don't really like children in general. Like, if I had never had children and I was just going by my experiences with other people's children then I would have thought they were loud and messy and annoying and who needs it?"

Once my boss was recounting her experience growing up with many siblings and cousins that were a constant presence in her mother's house and she said, "Raising children is no joke!" Which I found hilarious because she said it with such seriousness but with this glint her eye like a mother might get if she has spent the morning repeating "Find your shoes" until the words lost all meaning.

It's been a constant struggle for me as I enjoyed my children as people but I wasn't the kind of mother who got down on the floor and played barbies for hours. I wasn't even that kind of child. I remember once when we were living in the caravan and I asked my mother if she would play barbies with me and within minutes I realised it was the dullest thing I had ever done. Another time I asked her to make me 'a fairy' and she cut out part of an egg carton, flipped it over and drew some eyes on it and glued on some cardboard wings. I took this monstrosity to a tree in the garden and tried to pretend it was a genuine fairy but even at 5 years old I knew I was just a kid with a flipped over piece of egg carton. I lack the patience to really play games with children because I can't summon the right enthusiasm to act as though I'm really a terrified plastic triceratops running away from a T-Rex into…a dollhouse? What's going on? Wait, why is there a barbie version of Niall from One Direction in the dollhouse now? And why doesn't he have on a shirt?

Maybe it makes me a really crappy mother to not be able to do those kinds of games with kids but I try to make up for it in other ways by reading bedtime stories or I'm always happy to colour with them or play a board game. The best thing about tweens is they mostly stop playing the kinds of games I'm bad at. The worst thing about tweens is everything else. That was a joke. A little truth though. They are really tough.

. . .

My eldest daughter just bewildered me as a tween. She was heavily into female pop stars and her greatest aspirations in life were, in no particular order, to work in a café, to sing on stage, and to wear high heels. She would spend hours listening to music on her little stereo and singing along and making up dance routines and that was kind of cute except that you never really realise how inappropriate some lyrics are until you hear a child sing them. But there she was being all cute and I would wander up to her room and notice it was an absolute bombsite and she was actually dancing *on* her belongings because the floor was obscured by 'things' and I would say, "Hey, can you clean up your room?"

And she would just lose her mind. I think tweens have some kind of pre-puberty hormones going through them and it just makes them completely irrational. Just now my tween son slammed his hand against the table because I refused to let him have a day off school even though school only just starts back tomorrow after a two-week break. Now I'm more seasoned I just tell him to knock it off, but he had nothing on my eldest who fell to the floor, made snow angels in the mess while wailing and then picked up a rollerblade and pitched it at the wall. She kind of scared me a little. It made me want to go back to playing dinosaurs and barbies.

She would throw 'parties' every week. We were all invited, it was a big deal. The thing I found about girls is they love cutting up paper. I don't know why but they love it. My boys never cut up paper because they were too busy making swords out of every available thing and trying to stab unsuspecting family members with them, but my daughters just loved to cut up little bits of paper and leave them around the place. Many trees have died at my daughters' hands. My eldest daughter went through this horrible stage of throwing 'snow parties'. She would spend all day cutting out elaborate snowflakes and sticky taping them to her wall, the ceiling fan, the curtains and finally I guess she would get jack of cutting them out neatly and she would just start cutting lots and lots of small coin sized bits of paper and throwing them around her room for snow. Coin sized bits of paper are too big to vacuum and too small not to develop knee damage while you crawl around picking them up for hours, it was a real trial in my life. I wanted to be the cool mum who was on board with her daughter's creative need to throw parties but I just couldn't deal with the mess. It was around this point that I decided to shift the bedroom arrangement around and move the tidy daughter out of the room into her own room and put the two that loved mess in the same room. I can't even describe the horror of that room. Clothes everywhere, toys everywhere, play make up everywhere. And everywhere, *everywhere*, these little pieces of cut up paper. Finally, one Sunday afternoon I told them they had to clean it up and whatever was still on the floor after they went to school Monday morning would be put into trash bags and thrown in the bin. I had heard of other mothers using this technique to great success. I had resolutely refused to even look in the room but I could see from the hallway as I passed that the floor was still covered with mess and I was gleefully imagining how they were really going to learn a lesson about not putting things away when they came home and found all the stuff gone.

I dropped the kids at school and entered the room armed with garbage bags. As I started to pick my way through it, I realised something. Nothing on the floor was anything they wanted. What was on the floor? Clothes they had outgrown and didn't want anymore, cups they had forgotten to take to the kitchen, siblings toys that had made their way in there and rubbish. Hundreds of small pieces of papers. It was all either items to be passed down or donated, things that belonged to the siblings, crockery I needed to wash or rubbish to be thrown away. These two girls had gone through their mess and put away anything they wanted and left me to pick up all the stuff they didn't because what was the point of doing that themselves if I had already threatened to bag it all up for them? Mama didn't raise no idiots. Lazy kids, maybe, but no idiots.

One time I was having a particularly hard day because I was struggling with the constant tantrums and struggle of my then tween son and I felt like he genuinely hated me or just saved up all his bad behaviour for when he got home. At school, he always got excellent behaviour written on his report cards and all his teachers would tell me what a delight he was to have in the classroom and yet when he got home he would meltdown about absolutely everything. Even when I would try to do something nice for him he would just lose his mind. One day I might bring him home a lollipop while I was doing the grocery shopping and I would hand it to him and he would start complaining, "Why did you even buy me this? I didn't ask for anything. I don't want it. I don't even like lollipops." I was at my wits end.

    I said all this to my friend, who is a teacher and probably sees a lot of really rotten behaviour, and she said that he definitely didn't hate me, he probably didn't even know himself why he acted that way. She said that sometimes the day is just so overwhelming for kids and they hold it all together until they get home, to their safe space, where they feel like they are allowed to release it all to someone who will still love them afterwards. She said, "You are his safe space." While adults or even teenagers might come home after a hard day and tell you all the ways their day sucked by venting, or little kids may crawl into your lap and cry, tweens are at this really hard age where they feel too big to cuddle up to you but they don't have the words to tell you why their day was hard. They just explode. On the difficult days, where I feel like I need a long service leave holiday, I repeat those words to myself like a mantra, "Be the safe place, be the safe place." And I remember transition and know, this too, shall pass.

21st October 2017 – The Journals

Last night I went to film night at the high school to watch the awards and I was sitting in front of a bunch of girls who were critiquing everyone's appearance as they came on stage. I know, I know. So typical of teen girls. But they were actually awesome. They had not one negative thing to say. Every time someone came up they were all,

"She looks great."
"I love her."
"She has done such a great job."
"She looks fabulous tonight."

It was a running commentary of compliments. Girls raising girls up. I don't know who raised them but I'd like to shake their hand.

THE TEENAGER

I feel like I could write an entire book on teenagers alone. Having a teenager is a lot like having a newborn, in that you are presented with someone you love dearly but who is basically a stranger to you. They keep strange hours, are horrifically messy and when they talk, you often have no idea what they're saying. They break into tears inexplicably. They're driven by food. Some days we would tiptoe around our teens and the next find ourselves locked in a battle of wills over a party they wanted to go to. Whatever handle you think you have on parenthood, teenagers are sure to shake it up.

Yet, like a newborn, they are also incredible. One day, you'll be in the kitchen cooking dinner and your child will suddenly begin having this conversation with you that is genuinely interesting or funny or engaging on an adult level and you will be startled by how grown up and amazing they are. I remember when my son was graduating primary school and because he was on student council he had to MC the event. At the beginning of it all the kids came out across stage to music, doing little dances and I bawled like a baby because for some reason since I had children whenever a group of people is singing or dancing together I start sobbing. I don't know what it is. Even talking about a group of people singing together can make my eyes fill. So, there I am crying and my son comes out and walks across stage and he is beaming out at the crowd, waving and dancing. He is a pretty conservative kid. He always has been. He was never silly like the rest of us who would do ridiculous things like make paper bag masks, or create silly videos or just generally act the fool to make everyone else in the house laugh. He played, but you could see that he was always conscious of himself and how he might appear. But when he walked across the stage it all just fell away. He still looked like himself but there was…something. Something just under the surface that made me think, "Oh, there he is." It was like I caught this glimpse of the man he would grow into, just for a second.

You are not always going to get along with your teenager. You don't always get along with your children at any age but sometimes you will be really blown away by how much you really don't like them at that specific point in time. Like a tween, when you bear the brunt of their outbursts, teenagers will continue this trend. But you suddenly have very little leverage over them with which to regain the upper hand. If a small child is behaving in a horrible way you might say that they're having no screen time today. If a tween is misbehaving then maybe they miss out on something they really wanted to do. A teen doesn't give a shit. They secretly do but they'll act like the don't. They'll force themselves to not give a shit just to spite you. I can turn off the internet in a rage after my teenager was being horrible and suddenly he will open a book and pretend to read and act as though he gives no shits, he's all out of shits, in fact turn off the lights also, he always enjoyed candlelight, how quaint. The other kids will emerge from the woodwork like ants after sugar, "Mother, why is the internet off? When will it come back on? Why aren't you putting the internet back on now? What have we done for you to punish us so?" The teenager will sit on the couch listening to this knowing that his siblings will do the nagging for him. He just needs to bide his time and keep not giving shits.

You are going to lose your patience.

Losing your patience will happen repeatedly throughout your parenting journey but by the time you have a teenager it usually doesn't happen quite as often and when it does you suffer intense guilt, because they're really quite fragile, teenagers.

Recently, I woke up and decided to bake. Anyone that knows me is aware this is an event that should be regarded with either high suspicion or as a miracle. After a few hours, I had baked a vanilla cake with buttercream icing and slivered almonds, and followed up with some walnut brownies. I called out to the children that if they wanted a piece of cake they were welcome to come and get it. My teenage son calls out, "Ugh…I suppose I'll get a piece, just put in on a plate and bring it here."

I swallowed down my irritation at being ordered around like a servant and said, "How about, *you* come here and get your *own* cake." He slumped into the kitchen, slammed a plate down beside me and shoved a slice of cake on to it, took three steps, bit into the cake and then lost his mind because he didn't like the icing.

"This is horrible! Why would you make this? It's disgusting."

The two smaller children look up in confusion from their own cake, probably hoping he doesn't cause this friendly, baking mother to disappear entirely. I'm very, very good at not sweating the small stuff. I'm basically a pro at doing a couple of deep breaths, turning away and ignoring it but I think all that repressed rage just bottles up over time. Before I know what I'm doing, I stalked over to him and, like an overgrown toddler, I grab a fistful of the top of his cake, looked him dead in the face and say, "There. The icing is off."

He looks at me like I've grown a second head and scuttles off with his mangled piece of cake.

Look. These things happen. In fact, sometimes it's okay to show your kids that you aren't a paragon of patience and are, in fact, human yourself. If they think they can get away with being jerks all the time then you're going to raise an adult who is a jerk. If you can manage to be cool as a cucumber in all situations then absolutely do so. But if you do find yourself like my friend did once, flinging her daughter's book out a window during a car trip when her teen was being particularly obnoxious, then try not to beat yourself up too badly. The important thing is that at some point in the future, you go and explain why they behaved inappropriately…and apologise for your own reaction. So, I did find myself later on telling my son the appropriate way to respond in a social situation when you don't care for the icing on a cake.

"You may find you have to eat it. Or you can carefully remove the icing and eat the cake."

"Why can't I just say I don't like the icing?"

"Well, you can. But you have to say it in a polite way. Like, you might say the cake is delicious but the icing is a bit too sweet for you."

He looks at me dubiously, "What if I hate the cake?"

"Then you choose something else nice to say. Like you might say that it was lovely for them to bake for you and just eat a small amount to be polite. It's like when you were little and you would give me a drawing and I would tell you I really liked the colours. I didn't point out that your person only had 3 fingers and their hair was unrealistic. I was polite so I didn't hurt your feelings and you kept drawing. Sometimes it's about encouraging someone so they don't stop doing something they enjoy before they get good enough to make a really good cake."

"Okay. Well...I'm sorry."

"That's alright. I'm sorry for grabbing a handful of your cake."

I've found teenagers, for the most part, to be empathetic. Of course, they have their moments where they are just jerks but they also have moments where they can see you are a person, not just a mum, and so you might say, "Mate, can you take out the trash for me?" And he knows it's his sister's job and she should do it and only a year ago he would have said just that but now he can also see you're worn out from the day, he notices the flatness of your voice and the sigh in your words, so he just goes and does it himself because he doesn't want to add to your misery. It might happen slowly at first but it does seem to happen more and more.

People often say about parenting teenagers that you can't be their friend. *I'm your parent, not your friend.* In fact, I have said that before myself when I was feeling particularly furious about an argument I was having with my daughter. But, I think you have to be both. Sometimes you are going to have to be the parent, especially when something is dangerous or has the potential to be so. Like if your child wants to go for a walk after dark on their own, perhaps you have to say no. You have to be the parent in that situation. But then you need to be the friend and ask why they wanted to go for a walk in the dark. Are they feeling sad or fed up or upset and they just want to walk? Or are they trying to sneak a cigarette and want to slip down to the park to do that? And if they're trying to sneak a cigarette then are they feeling like they want a cigarette because they're feeling sad or fed up or upset? You won't know if you don't ask. They might not tell you but if they do, don't dismiss what they say.

Exactly like when you were parenting your toddler, teenagers will want to do things on their own. And like when you were parenting your toddler, sometimes you will know that is not going to work out. Your job is to give them enough rope to explore while still placing in enough safe boundaries that they come home relatively unscathed. They might go to parties and drink. Smoke weed. Have sex. And all of this is alarming because you know all those situations are fraught with danger. And then some wiseass called the Department of Transport decides that they're old enough to drive and you have a whole new thing to worry about.

High school can be an incredibly difficult and toxic experience for many people. You might know that in 10 years time that problem will seem small and insignificant, that they will survive, but for your teenager just now, it is very hard and very awful. Imagine that kind of pressure, you're in school being told if you don't do very well you may screw up the rest of your life right now, you've got hormones rushing through your body, your face is breaking out, your boyfriend is a lying asshole, your best friend is actually kinda mean and in the middle of it someone is offering you a very badly mixed drink that's so strong you could stand a spoon up in it. Add to that all the stuff that still screws us up as adults, societal pressure to look a certain way or act a certain way and to top it off, your brain isn't even finished developing yet. It's a wonder all of us aren't in therapy just because we had to go through being teenagers.

Teenagers are going to have sex. I could give you a thousand reasons why I got pregnant beyond the obvious. I've had a lot of children, planned and not and if you ever think that the short talk teenagers get on sex education is going to save your children from changing nappies before they've graduated high school, you are sorely mistaken. In a large cohort of girls, I didn't get pregnant because I was the only irresponsible one; we were all irresponsible. It's just that it happened to me. You can clinically tell teenagers how pregnancy happens, you can tell them to always use condoms, but it's not enough. It's not nearly enough. Sometimes I don't think I got a good grasp on exactly how my body was working until I was 24 and trying to fall pregnant with my son. When I was in high school, in grade 8 we got two days of awful sex education. These involved one day where they piled all of us together and showed us a slideshow which included a flaccid penis drawn in cartoon, becoming more erect as the slides went on. I can't really remember much else because we were all absolutely mortified. It simply isn't a good learning environment. No one told us where to go to get condoms. I'm not talking about the store, because for a 15-year-old walking into a store and buying condoms is an ordeal. I'm talking about free clinics that ask no questions, where you get to go into a private room and a nurse might actually talk to you properly about the ins and outs of keeping yourself safe, gift you a bag of condoms or the pill and instruct you on how to use them. Or test you for STDs. Because I got a baby, but it could have been a lot worse.

Teenagers need support. Many of them, most of them even, aren't going to ask for it. They aren't going to ask you to put condoms on the shopping list. They might be embarrassed or scared to ask you to take them to the GP to get the pill. They might not want to talk to you about a rash in their private areas. You need to keep the lines of communication open. You need to talk openly as possible about sex and all that comes with it with them, well before they're ready and tell them they can always come to you – no judgements allowed – about any problems they're having. But you also need to provide them with the tools to do it themselves in case they aren't the kind of kids that will come to you off their own back. Teach them how to catch public transport and give them the numbers for helplines. Tell them where free clinics are located and get them their own Medicare card. Tell them of bulk billing GPs that are local to you. Explain birth control options available and their pros and cons, or even just stop into your local GP and pick up a few pamphlets to leave on their bed. Buy condoms and put them in the bathroom cupboard and replace them when they run low. You may still ask questions because you still want them to be safe, but check your own emotions at the door. When my eldest daughter came to me in her late teens and asked me to take her to get the morning after pill, I felt my stomach fall into my shoes. I wanted to ask a thousand questions (and hear none of the answers) and I wanted to lecture, but I had always told her to come to me so I said "of course"... and then I went and sequestered myself in the garage with a shot of whiskey and placed my head between my knees for a few moments to steady myself. So, I think your questions should always be focused about their safety. Are they okay with everything? Do they feel comfortable and respected by their partner? Are they ensuring their partner is comfortable and respected by them? Do they have any questions? These are the important things.

I've been grateful repeatedly that I'm not a teenager in the world now. High school was hard enough, people were mean enough, without the safety net of home being ripped away. And in today's society with social media so ingrained in our teenager's life even home isn't always the safe haven it should be. I can't imagine all the stupid things I did being on the internet forever. Or all the stupid things I *didn't* do but the gossip still went around that I *did* do being on the internet forever.

When I was in high school there was one girl who for the entire of grade 9 kept threatening to hit me. Anytime I walked nearby she would say it loudly to her friends or to me and there was no real reason for it because as far as I could see I hadn't done anything except exist. Honestly, I don't know what happened to her that she was so damaged she felt she needed someone to hate this badly – and believe me, it's taken me years to finally be that zen about it and realise it really was a 'her' issue. On the first day of grade 10 she came up to me and said, "We're okay now. Now I hate her." And she pointed to my friend who became the next target. I was so stunned that I said nothing and just stood there, blinking. Was I supposed to thank her for the kindness of deciding that this non-existent problem had now been rectified? Should we sit down and braid each other's hair? I wanted to tell her categorically to fuck right off and keep on going but I said nothing because I was so damn relieved I wasn't going to get jumped outside the toilet blocks for breathing. I have no doubt that had social media and smart phones been around during that time of my life the pervasive feeling of being prey would have extended into my personal messages, she'd have started group chats of exclusion, she would have left hate messages on all my Instagram posts. I cannot imagine running that gauntlet, day in and day out and never feeling like I was really safe or that it was okay just to be who I was.

Bullying is such a major issue for our teenagers and we can throw all the 'Bullying No Way' days we like but make no mistake, despite these initiatives, bullying is still almost epidemic. And our children are dying over it. A brief look through the internet will reveal pages and hotlines both parents and children can access to help them deal with and overcome bullying, as well as recommendations of how to approach schools to assist you with this. I would strongly urge parents whose children are in the midst of it to find them support in the form of a counsellor or psychologist so they have an impartial person to talk to as bullying is still one of the major causes of our teenagers taking their own lives and I have read far too many heart wrenching posts from parents whose children have attempted suicide and are seeking a way to keep their child here on earth. We also need to teach our children to advocate for their peers, to stand up and call out bad behaviour and be inclusive to those who are being targeted. Some children may be reluctant to do this, even children who are incredibly empathetic, because of fear of being targeted themselves or because they're naturally introverted. If your child doesn't feel safe to say something directly to the bully then encourage them to privately seek out support for their peers by telling a parent, a teacher or the school guidance officer so that they can follow this up. I feel this is necessary both for the child being targeted and the bully themselves because for bullies the actions are a symptom of whatever lies beneath the surface. I mean, sometimes kids are just jerks, just like adults can be jerks sometimes, but bullying isn't a once off, offhand mean comment, it's constant harassment of one person and children who are safe and well-adjusted don't go around destroying other people. Something is wrong. That girl from my story above? She wasn't a bad person, I had known her since we were 5 years old and I knew that she could be kind and funny and a generally cool person even though we had never really been friends. But something was really wrong. Which isn't to say how she behaved was okay and as a teenager I did not have the emotional fortitude to explore her reasons why, I just wanted it to stop. *She* probably didn't have the emotional fortitude to figure it out. Adults needed to figure it out to help the both of us. If you find out your child is bullying someone else, seek out the cause while being firm about the behaviour stopping. It can be really hard to hear that your child is doing something nasty to someone else but how you deal with this now can make a lasting difference for both your child and the other child. Seek help and break the cycle.

Despite all the temper tantrums, the fear of trying to guide your child through these years safely and the worry you are going to lose your own mind, teenagers are wonderful. They inject a colour into your life. They're still children so they can be silly and crazy and messy and on any given day you might find them curled up on the couch watching a Disney movie, swanning out the door looking like they're off to a photoshoot or standing in the kitchen looking like a homeless urchin. These years are hard. They will test you. You will still find you have no earthly idea what you're doing and at times you will be certain you have made a terrible error and they'll be lying on a therapist's couch one day recounting the time you picked up the dishes they refused to do and pitched them straight out the window and on to the lawn. Sometimes it will feel like you're in a relationship with a partner that you can't stand and if they were your husband, you would be filling out divorce forms right now. It doesn't last forever. Everything passes. You will have moments where you're playing a board game with them at the kitchen table or chatting in the car on the way to dropping them at a mate's place or just hanging out with them and you will think, "You're actually a really cool person." You'll think how they're funny and kind to others and how they have awesome taste in music or they genuinely care about the environment and you'll be amazed at how incredible they are. Savour that. You did a pretty good job, mama.

STATISTICALLY UNSAFE

Years ago, when my daughter was about 18 and worked in a fast food place she had an unpleasant experience with a male customer who was being lewd and gross. I won't get into what happened because it was her story and is not mine to tell. However, when her friend (who was living with us at the time) and I were going to pick her up from work and her friend told me that my daughter had texted her about it during the day I was worried she would come out really shaken and not want to go back. To the contrary she brushed it off as nothing. Initially I was relieved. And then I was mad. Because of the world we live in, even now, and because she is a woman this kind of thing will undoubtedly happen to her time and time again, and at 18 she had already accepted that. She had already become used to it. She already failed to be shocked by it.

I have four daughters, five including her friend who lived with us and who I regard as a daughter. I think of the statistics and this terrifies me. When I was relaying the statistics for sexual assault against women to a male friend – 1 in 6 women are raped – he said, "That can't be right. That can't be." It's not that he doesn't believe me. It's that he can't wrap his mind around the sheer enormity of it. When I discussed his reaction with my therapist she said she felt the stats were grossly underestimated and she would put it more like 6 out of 10.

Here is the thing. I'm outraged at this. I am. I am a woman who has shared article about the unfairness of victim blaming. I am a woman who has been enraged by news stories or sound bites from people that talk about, "How to stay safe." Because fuck you, that's why. We shouldn't have to alter our daily lives so men don't rape us. Men should just stop raping us. I know that. I hate that I have to tell my daughters how to navigate this world by altering their behaviour because I know I shouldn't have to. But I do. I do it anyway because I want them to come home. And you know what I hate more than the fact I do that? I hate that I don't even have to. Because they already know. Instinctively, they already know. Like some strange evolutionary trait attached to the second X chromosome, my daughters already understand and avoid walking too close to the alley so they don't get pulled in but not too close to the street so they don't get ripped into a car. They already know to watch drinks. Walk in groups. Text your friends. Make sure your girlfriends are in your line of sight at a party. I thought of how women know those things, fear those things, do those things and felt for a second like I could feel all those wounds from the women that came before me encoded somewhere in my own DNA. Sometimes, in sheer desperation I hand my daughters pieces of other women's stories as though by invoking the spirits of these women who never made it home I will somehow help my daughter to return to me. I can't reconcile these two parts of myself. The part of me that wants to give them the tools to help them come home unscathed and the part of me that hates myself for having to do it.

I remember when I first read The Lovely Bones by Alice Sebold and I had to put it down and walk away for a time because I realised, I was Susie Salmon. Or I could have been. When she was walking across the field and every molecule in her body was telling her to get the hell outta dodge but she didn't want to be impolite so she crawled down into the hole? I would have done that. I've always been a shocking people pleaser. I would have gotten in the car, gone into the dark room, lay still, stayed quiet, kept secrets because I wouldn't want to offend, I wouldn't want to seem rude. Sometimes I think back on some of the completely careless things I did as a teenager and my blood runs cold. I remember going to the park with my friend one night so we could sneak cigarettes and a car with a couple of guys in it pulled up and they came over and chatted to us for awhile and then offered for us to go for a drive with them. I have no idea what possessed us to get in the car, but we did and they drove us up to this housing estate that was just being built, totally empty, no one for miles. We were completely vulnerable but they just smoked some weed and then dropped us back at the park about an hour later. There were men who followed us home from parties, walking behind us the whole way through unlit underpasses. There were men who catcalled, men who asked us for kisses as we were walking home from a friend's house and happened to pass by their open garage. Men who offered us beers, men who offered us rides, men who asked us if they could come home with us. Which isn't to say that we made it to womanhood unscathed. Just that we are alive. Just that we came home. I kept thinking of all those times and wondering how on earth I was going to keep my girls alive.

When all of this happened, I took this to my women friends who have daughters and I said, "What do you do? How do you teach your girls to stay safe and not hate yourself for saying it?" A lot of mothers said they do the same thing, the repeat the same things we were told, things we learned, things our girlfriends told us over drinks. One friend told me how when she was a uni student and had no money to catch public transport home from work late at night, her roommate taught her to wear caps to tuck her hair up into, baggy clothes, things that hid her figure to help make her less conspicuous. Everyone had a story. Every one of those mothers expressed their own dismay at repeating the same things that made them angry when they read them as quotations from law enforcement when yet another woman would turn up dead in a park. I remember reading once that women don't text their friends because that text message is going to keep them safe, that's like wishing on a dandelion. Women are documenting their deaths. So they know where to find us. So they know when it happened. So they know where we were when we were taken. And yet, it isn't even strangers that are most likely to hurt us. The biggest danger to girls and women is the ones who we trust. They are the monsters we know.

I don't know the right thing to tell your girls. I don't know if I would ever counsel a mother to not hand over those pieces of wisdom, those little tales of caution, because sometimes a paper shield feels better in the hand than no shield at all. I do know that we need to tell them to be their own champions.

Our daughters need to know they can shout, they can take up space, they can be rude. Rude is better than dead. Light a fire, keep it burning.

I also know we need to also talk to our boys. We need to teach them from very young about consent, about advocacy, about the statistics. Saying no is a no. Saying no with body language is a no. Saying yes and then changing your mind means it's a no now. No still means no even if you're married. If you have to really cajole her before she says yes, it's a no. Anything that isn't a hell yes? That's a no. That sulking after a no makes you an asshole. Time and again I hear women try to tell their tales to men and they'll tell us how they aren't like that, 'not all men'. And then I hear women say, "Listen to us." Because we still want you to hear us when we tell you we are scared, that these things have happened to us. We need to teach our boys to listen, to give us the space to talk. I think as mother's we can start small. We can raise our girls so they feel comfortable at an early age saying no to physical affection.

"Would you like to give Mummy a hug goodnight?"

"No."

"Okay, no worries. Have a good sleep! I love you."

We can teach our boys, "Your sister doesn't want to be hugged right now. Not everybody likes to be hugged all the time. Just give her some space for now."

A male friend once told me that if he is ever walking along alone and a woman is walking along alone, he crosses the street and walks on the other side so she doesn't have to. Maybe she wouldn't have cared, maybe she wasn't scared, but chances are without even thinking of it, she had already done a quick self-assessment of the situation. My daughter's boyfriend told me that he pulled his car up once on the street across from his house and three girls were walking down and they looked at him and then exchanged worried glances with each other, and he was worried they would think he was wanting to harass or harm them so he quickly got his bag and made it obvious he lived there. He said that he feels he often changes his behaviour also, as a result, after he turned 14 and grew tall he avoided going to the park to hang out unless it was completely empty, he monitors friends' behaviours and tells them to settle down if they're getting rowdy as he is aware of what they look like as a group and that they might seem threatening. I cannot tell you how much I appreciate these efforts, I could tell while talking to him that these things weigh on his mind. But I was also aware that while he worried about people *thinking* he *might* be a threat, women worry about the threat. We need more men who are consciously and actively aware. We want you as our allies.

4th December 2015 – The Journals

E had her kindergarten graduation tonight. They all had a disco and the kids got given light up cat ears and their room had been decorated with hundreds of little lights. My little girl was so shy at the beginning of the year she wouldn't talk to a single person, so I thought we would spend the night glued to the wall just watching everyone else, but she really surprised me and wanted to dance. She danced next to her friend and her friend's mother and keep tugging at my sleeve to whisper to me, "Can you spin me around?" And we would whirl her around in the air so that her hair flew out behind her and she giggled. I remember when she started kindergarten I was so nervous I had to get a friend to drive me to drop her off because I was sure I was going to spend the entire trip home crying about how my baby is growing up. Then next year she will go to school and before I know it she won't be tugging at my sleeve to spin her anymore. She will be dancing on her own.

GRADUATION

When we first moved back to Brisbane we all seemed to spend the next year in some kind of strange shell shock. I didn't have plans, none of us had plans. We moved fast, rehoming chickens and goats, doing trips to the local tip, my eldest daughter listed most of our furniture on the local Buy, Swap, Sell page, we packed up the house and I got a lease on a place in Brisbane without ever having seen it. In two weeks time, we had an entire new life. We had to quickly book the children into school and for the first time I had to deal with catchments and realised our options were quite limited. The older three got booked into the local high school and the two boys into the primary next to it.

My second eldest had always been a quiet achiever. She did well in school without really having to put in a lot of effort, she kept a few close friends because sometimes she was hard to get to know. She kept her own counsel. She has always been a reader, a lover of video games and pop culture. She was stoic, I hadn't seen her cry since she was 5 years old.

. . .

When she began high school at this new place she would wake up every morning and not want to go. She never lied and said she was sick. She didn't try to get out of it, she just would sadly get dressed and the sparkle left her eyes. One morning I found her crying as she was getting ready and I felt like I was destroying my child. She never cried and if she was crying something was very wrong. So, I took her out of school and just let her breathe. For the first few weeks she lay in bed, reading a book or watching tv and doing not much at all. I have discovered that children rarely do nothing for long. Soon enough, she emerged and would sit at the kitchen table and draw. Drawing turned to sculpture and then sculpture turned to sewing and sewing turned to special effects make up. We talked about what she would do now, I told her she had to do something, it didn't have to be school but it needed to be *'something'*, and we found a Diploma of Specialist Make Up that had a special effects component. This shy girl would catch the train every day and go to her lessons in the city. She took classes with adults, she would walk the city at lunchbreaks and visit bookstores. She would ride the train home with different make up every day and she didn't seem shy at all.

When she finished the Diploma, I broached the topic of high school again. I was surprised that she agreed to give it a go and we compromised and decided she would try for six months and if it wasn't for her, then it wasn't, and we would find something else. It was difficult to re-enrol her, we handed in our forms and then had to have a meeting with the Principal and Guidance Officer which felt remarkably like a job interview where you weren't really qualified for the position. They seemed unimpressed with her previous grades, the Guidance Officer said that it would be too hard for her to do senior and that had she considered Tafe or a certificate?

"I've already done a Diploma," my daughter said.

The Guidance Officer made a noise in the back of her throat. We went back and forth, the Guidance Officer voicing her reluctance, her concerns and me assuring her that this was they path we wanted to take. Eventually, I pushed the matter until they agreed to enrol her promising to keep a careful eye on her grades. My daughter and I walked out of the school silently before I finally burst out, "I think they think you're stupid!"

"Oh, my god! Right?" my daughter exclaimed.

But they didn't know my girl. And 18 months later she was cleaning up in the film night awards, preparing for her final exams and organising a formal dress.

Whether or not your children pursue an academic pathway or otherwise there will be this moment when you realise you are done. Of course, as a parent you are never really done. But it's like a 'done' feeling. They're grown. They've made it. *You've* made it. All those times you did the school runs, all those end of year concerts, the parent teacher meetings, the uniforms and lunches. All those times you looked after them when they were sick. All those drives out to friends' houses. All those times you didn't know how you were going to afford school fees or thought that the booklist companies were going to bankrupt you. And suddenly, there you are. You both survived, relatively unscathed and whole and neither of you in desperate need of therapy just this second, which is a relief. The difference with graduation is that you have a definitive 'end' and there is some kind of benchmark with which to gauge your 'doneness'.

. . .

I was a wreck. I actually *was* having therapy at the time, although it wasn't related to my children or the fact one was graduating and just because I'm constantly living on the verge of hysteria about one thing or another. Unfortunately for me, my therapist also had a child graduating at the same school and so I was fairly certain after seeing my emotional breakdown in the audience she was about to bail me up outside the hall and demand we book in a session that afternoon. It was the damn singing again. Lord, save me from groups of people singing together, I can't cope. I was the mother, standing on the chair with my camera, photographing her daughter walking across the stage to collect her graduation certificate, bawling my eyes out. I just had to pray the autofocus on the camera had my back because I couldn't see a damn thing. They were just so full of joy and hope and possibility and right at that moment it didn't matter what they did after this day, on *this* day they were the doctors, the politicians, the artists, the journalists, the teachers, the business owners of the future. They were all of our collective hope that we sent out into the world when we decided to have children. They signified our dreams and our wishes that this world would be a better place. One of the kids was dancing through the aisles while he sang and the parents were all clapping and laughing and that hall just felt so full of love and joy that it nearly broke my heart with the beauty of it. I cried and cried.

After the graduation, all the kids went home to get ready for their formal. We sat around and she curled her hair and she did her own make up because she had a Diploma in it, after all. Her dress was a long, fitted black strapless with gold detailing along the bodice. She wore it with chunky high black boots because she's been bucking trends since 1999, no strappy heels for this lass. The whole family came to the house, the boys in button up shirts and trousers and the girls in dresses in varying shades of blue because even when we don't try to colour co-ordinate, we do. Her dad came along with his partner and little girl and we all went down to the high school so that all the parents could see their kids all dolled up and get photos before they left for the event.

It's always a little awkward when her dad and I get thrust together at these kinds of events. We had been apart for longer than we had been together and you once knew each other better than anyone but you don't really know each other at all anymore. There is all this water under the bridge because you once told each other you loved each other and you also fought and yelled and hurt each other probably as bad as any human being can hurt another person's heart. You know all this but it somehow doesn't matter anymore because the years have healed those wounds until they're just a part of you. I caught his eye and I smiled and hoped he knew it was because no matter what, no matter how it ended, none of it mattered because both of us just loved the girl we were there for, looking so beautiful in her long black dress, her golden hair falling down her back in curls. She shone. She was radiant. I could barely believe something so beautiful could have come from me.

I just cried and cried.

9th January, 2017 – The Journals

I've raised an adult. An actual person. Someone I gave birth to and watched take her first steps and say her first word and I saw her on her first day of school and watched her in school plays and saw her off to her first day of high school and witnessed her first heartbreak over a boy and drove her to her first day of work. Now she is here making these grown up decisions and last year she voted for the first time. Soon she will move out and that's scary and amazing. You never remember the 'lasts'. I can't remember the last time I carried her in when she fell asleep in the car or the last time she skinned her knee and demanded I kiss it better. Mothers are the keeper of firsts.

I was 16 when I had her. Younger than she is now. She is good and kind and helpful and a hard worker and so goddamn amazing that I can't believe she came from me. And sometimes I still feel like I'm 16 and I still have no idea what I'm doing and yet I fluked my way through this journey and here she is – arrived. Done. Raised. Flying. And this person? She is my friend. She is a wonderful friend. She is someone I would want to hang around and have my back and really that's the greatest thing, I think. To have raised someone you would want as your friend. I'm so proud of her. It's like, one day you look up and they're walking out the door with their bags on their way to work and they've packed a lunch because they're trying to save money and budget and that's such a grown-up thing that it just takes your breath away and you think, "Oh. I'm done here. You'll be okay. You're on your own now."

You don't remember the lasts. But I remember the first time I looked up and saw my daughter standing in front of me as a woman. Smart, brave, kind, fierce, together. Amazing.

LEAVING HOME

She fell in love. That was how it happened. The house was too small of course and the children were too many but we probably could have all put up with that, we were so used to living in the laps of each other, if it wasn't for the fact that she fell in love. He is a good man. He works hard and he is ambitious and he is endlessly patient with her siblings and he is funny and when they cook dinner they dance and sing in the kitchen. She had just gotten a job in reception she had had to hustle to get, writing Erin Brockovitch style cover letters until someone was so impressed that they hired her. She has never done things the easy way, this daughter of mine, but she is tenacious, she knows her own mind and she beats a path to where she wants to go. I could see that she was getting ready to go before she said the words.

She left the same day as her sister's 18th birthday party. She was wearing a red dress. Her arms were filled with boxes that held her clothes, her books, her childhood. I hugged her goodbye and it all felt a little anticlimactic. I remembered when I left home when I was 15 and pregnant with her and my mother had gotten my brother's ready for school and herself ready for work and had said goodbye like it was any other day. And I was *fine*, I was completely okay until my grandfather came over and loaded up his van with my stuff and as we were driving away I burst into tears. He glanced over at me and then did a double take and said, "What the bloody hell is going on? What are you crying for?" I think he was alarmed at my emotional reaction and didn't quite know how to deal with it himself.

"I'm sad!" I wailed.

"Well, what for?"

"I'm just sad to be leaving!"

He looked hard at the road and was silent for awhile, "Well, you're just going a few minutes up the road. You can come back whenever you like."

I'm not sure why leaving always feels anticlimactic for me, like we should all be cutting off locks of each other's hair and making oaths and instead you just wave them off and make plans for next week. Then I found her sheety.

When she was a baby she had this port-a-cot that she loved. It was the only thing she would sleep in. When we went to my mother-in-laws house and stayed the night she wouldn't sleep in that port-a-cot, she had to have her own. It was this old one that had been a hand me down and it was kind of awkward to take anywhere as the smallest it collapsed to was the size of its base which meant you had to have a really big boot to go anywhere but fortunately we owned an old ford falcon which was built like a tank and roomy, even though it was the ugliest shade of orange you had ever seen in your life. We only had one sheet that fit this cot properly so I would wash and dry it on the same day in between naps and put it back on. She had always been a tummy sleeper from the moment she could roll over and she would flip herself on to her stomach, grab a handful of this sheet and pop her thumb in her mouth (something that would later cost me $7000 in orthodontic fees) and go straight to sleep. One day when she had just begun to walk I stripped all the sheets and had them in a pile in the hall waiting for the wash when she picked up this sheet and carried it around and it was then I realised that she wasn't attached to the cot at all. It was the damn sheet. I remade the cot with a different sheet but handed her that one to hug and she was never apart from it after that. It was the ugliest cuddle toy you can ever imagine. It wasn't even new when we got it, it was another hand me down. It was soft and thin with wear but once upon a time it must have been fairly high quality. She carried it around for years, to daycare and kindergarten, it got holes in it and I patched them with pretty floral scraps from her old dresses and one time, horribly, it caught on fire when it was dropped too close to the old bar heater which resulted in poor sheety losing 1/3 of himself and an end to use of bar heaters. When he would get washed she would sit in front of the dryer watching him go around and around, chanting in her little high pitched doll voice, "Sheeeeeet. Sheeeeeet."

When she got older she still kept him under her pillow where she could reach up and hold him while she slept and finally when she hit about 16 he ended up in a box in the top of her cupboard, which is where I found him when I was moving my middle daughter into her sister's old room the afternoon she left home. I held this old raggedy thing in my hands and felt the all these memories wash over me like the tide. I sent her a text with a photo of sheety and a joking message about "How could you?" and she immediately text me back, "Omg, omg! I didn't mean to leave him! I thought he was in the boxes!" I almost didn't want to give him back to her. I felt like I wanted to keep him under my pillow, like I would carry him around with me and he could sit beside me on drives to work and when I died they would bury me with this awful little mangled sheet. Motherhood. It makes you crazy and breaks your heart and one day you find yourself unreasonably emotionally attached to a decades old piece of linen.

I did feel bereft after her leaving. I took to my friends with older kids and asked what they did when their kids left home to stay connected and they all had different advice, but mostly they had sympathy and assured me that it will all become the new normal and you will figure out what works for you in your own way. We started by having weekly dinners and she and her partner would come by after work once a week and then we got busy and sometimes we don't see them for a few weeks but when they do come over the house brims over with joy and laughter and I know we are going to all be just fine.

Before your child leaves home there will be a myriad of things you can help them with to prepare them for the world. It's things we do every day but we don't really think about it, but when they leave home they need to know how to do it for themselves. Some of it may be things you have already helped them learn, like how to put on a load of washing or clean a bathroom but if you haven't, it is worth teaching them in their teens. While some children have a good grasp, some kids may not, particularly if they're fresh out of high school and moving away for university. I think I could have gone missing for 3 days when my eldest was 15 and she would have managed to keep the house running but I know my fourth child would just exist on cereal and Xbox and die of malnutrition at the same age. I have some work to do there. Think about all the adult things you do every day that you manage on autopilot but your child may not have had the need to know. Some of the important things are:

- Basic household cleaning
- Meal planning
- Grocery shopping on a budget
- Cooking
- How to pay a bill
- How to catch public transport and read the timetables
- Basic car maintenance
- How to sew back on a shirt button, or hem a pair of pants/skirt
- How to book a doctor's appointment
- How to check their immunisation status and know when they need boosters
- How to lodge a tax return
- How to write a resume and cover letter
- How to write a resignation letter
- How to vote (please do teach them this one)
- How to manage/save money
- How to open/close a bank account
- To trust their instincts
- When to call for help

This is by no means a comprehensive list but it should help you get started. Life is bloody hard, they're going to make mistakes and sometimes you may find you still have to take up an oar and help row for a bit but you can prepare them as best you can. This is what this entire journey has been. From the moment you taught them to crawl, you've been teaching them to get somewhere without you. Now, that day has arrived.

Sometimes they are going to do things you absolutely don't agree with. For example, when my eldest first moved out she got a personal loan for a car. I know lots of people get loans for cars but I am the kind of person who just bums around in whatever car is safe and affordable. My cars are workhorses. They get washed once a year and usually when I only absolutely have to. I think this is primarily because when I was growing up we would drive whatever car my grandparents had just upgraded from. My dad would bring home this car that had been running around the farm and they never had air con and they might have a dent somewhere, and I have vivid memories of my mother having to spray WD40 into the engine every morning before dropping us at school and driving herself to work. I'm sure they could have gone and gotten a loan and bought a really nice car but my dad was the kind of person who really resented having a mortgage because he couldn't understand why they couldn't just buy their first home with cash, so we just didn't do that. So, when she said she was getting a loan for a car I was very dubious. But she went and bought her little pink car and not quite two years later she paid it out early and it worked out just fine for her. It can be very difficult to let go of the reins in those instances but you have to step back, breathe, and hope for the best.

. . .

Once I read a book and in it there was a long list of things every woman should know. I was at a stage in my life where I was pretty sure that if I were playing a video game I would have hit the reset button so I read this list avidly in the hopes it would give me some pointers on how to turn things around. Everything in it was very practical, sensible stuff but right at the end it had, "How to grow flowers". Perhaps the author meant literal flowers, I don't know, but I took it metaphorically in that, you need to have some colour. You need to know how to seek it out and find the gratitude in each day. Your child absolutely needs to know how to budget and BPay a bill but they also need to know how to grow their own flowers. You have to keep something back that is just yours, that doesn't belong to your boss, or your kids, or your landlord, or even your partner. It's something that you do just for you. Maybe it's running or singing or throwing pottery or maybe it's actually growing literal flowers for you, but whatever it is, it needs to belong to you and it should make time slip away when you do it.

When I used to take photos, I would sometimes feel like the walls were closing in on me and I would bundle the kids outside and I would take my camera and just shoot. I would shoot the chickens scratching under the trees and the chamomile growing through the cracks in the bricks of the flower bed and the goats eating the grapevines. Two hours later we would come back inside with red cheeks from the cold and I would have grass stains on my knees and leaves in my hair but I felt like someone had breathed the life back into me. That's what growing flowers does. It blows away the cobwebs in your mind and makes you feel like everything might be okay after all. Teach your children to grow their own flowers.

24th July 2016 – The Journals

I made a conscious effort lately to pull out the camera and take photos of life. Not posed images, but the images where the Doritos are still in a packet on the kitchen table and the kids' faces are illuminated by their phones. The images where we are in the car or there is a smudge of dirt on a five-year olds cheek. The ones where I set the timer and hop back into place and find out later the focus totally missed the mark and the table I leaned it on is in focus and we are but a kaleidoscope of colours. We could be anyone.

Wrinkles. Blemishes. Hair messed up. Sweatpants.

Life.

I've fallen in love with these images. Their imperfections and the impermanent of it. Just a second in time, gone. I feel like a journalist, like a historian. Every time I press the shutter I think – this will mean something someday. These will be the images that hold my attention. There is no bullshit here, no trappings.

When I use to shoot, clients would often say, "We like unposed photos." And I would have to explain to them that EVERY image in my portfolio was posed. Every single one. The ones that looked candid were really just disguised poses.

"Hold on to Daddy's leg so he doesn't run away."

"Can you kiss Mummy on the cheek?"

"Pretend you like each other."

Laughter.

Click. Click. Click.

A friend once sent me a text from nowhere last year when I was in the depths of depression and asked how I was. We hadn't talked in over 12 months but she used to be one of my best friends and had been my confidante for years. Then life got in the way and we drifted apart and I felt like a shitty friend and the more time that went by the more I felt embarrassed about reconnecting with her. I don't know how she knew to reach out to me then. I cried when I got her message which was simply little more than, "I'm thinking of you." I apologised for being a crappy friend and she told me there was nothing to be sorry for – which of course made me cry more. I lay my sorrows at her feet and told her I couldn't stop crying, I cried all day for weeks at just about everything and she said to me, "Life is awkward and precious."

I loved that so much I wrote it down and went back to it every now and then. Because it is awkward. The mess, the reality, the indignities. The laughs where you snort during them. The tears that smear your eye makeup. The sweat. The blood. The sex. The love.

And, my god. It is precious.

OMEGA

For awhile now, my grandfather has been descending into the darkness of Alzheimer's. It strips him away in layers until he is something less substantial. When he would 'show up' it was in bits and pieces of himself, but almost never in entirely the same way. He became a spectre of himself…and that was the hardest thing. It was such a gradual slide that one day all of a sudden, I found myself beginning to cry, the raw, sobbing gasps of grief, despite the fact he was still here, because, he isn't. He slips into shadow even while he sits with us.

As he disappeared, my grandmother began the process of packing up their house to sell, with the intention of purchasing a stand-alone unit at an aged care facility, something easier to manage, as she was doing everything on her own now. We gathered on weekends, sometimes all of us, sometimes only a couple, washing walls and packing away items. It was the strangest time. We are still laughing and joking because we can't help it when we are together but Nanna is giving us the things we said we always wanted when she died like she's getting in early, and my grandfather is asking me tentatively if that baby I'm holding is mine when it's actually my cousins but he just doesn't remember. It was like a really weird party. And in the middle of it, my grandfather slipped and broke his pelvis. He went to the hospital and then to a nursing home and he never came home again. Suddenly, Nanna had to pack up the house, go to court to become his enduring power of attorney so she could legally sell the house and move herself to the unit, close to my grandfather. I watched my mother, aunts and my cousins rally around my grandparents. It felt like someone had started the drums. Someone had blown the horn. Someone had called and we had answered. Family are these invisible threads that tie you to one another, so gossamer fine that you don't even notice they're there until that moment where you are needed and they burn bright and red. I could no more ignore the call than the beat of my own heart.

I kept exploring those ties. The ones that shape us, make us, guide us, break us. The ones that forge us.

I began writing this memoir the summer my daughter turned 21. I raided the bookshelves, dragging out photo albums, revisiting my beginnings, shocked by my own youth, marvelling at the dynamic creatures that I somehow managed to create. I opened the chest in the living room and pulled out the tiny outfits that reside within, holding them to my chest and remembering when they were once filled with the small, sweet heft of a newborn. I found drawings and school photos and old birthday cards. I took out the quilt I was given when Riley was born and lay it in my lap. I held up a painted handprint of my son's, pressing my palm to his.

I felt like a time traveller, skipping through the years. One moment I'm in the SCN, so real I can almost smell the antiseptic soap, the next it's the heat of summer in my bathroom and I am hearing my midwife tell me, 'just one more push' as my son slid into her hands. Then, suddenly, back here in suburbia, a silent house, the cat stretching lazily in front of me. Sometimes the story would stop, I would pace back and forth trying to summon a past incarnation of myself to speak and other times I would collapse on the sofa at the end of the day and announce I spent too long in 1998 today.

Mothers. I think I have had several of them, each gifting me with parts of herself. My grandmother – who I now see under the clothes line pinning sheets and myself, six years old, telling her stories. My aunties, one of them swimming with me under a summer dawn, teaching me to kick my legs like a frog. My other aunt, like a sister, like the godmother she was named to be, who played games with me and then held my secrets to her chest. My daughter's grandmother, a woman full of unconditional love, a teller of stories who blessed me with her openness, a woman full of energy and friendship. And my own Mother. A pillar. A lighthouse. Constant.

I wonder what my I gifted my children.

. . .

I cannot tell you the right way to be a mother. Even now, I do not know. I do know some things though. That family answer the call. That the magic of motherhood lives in the details. And that a story is a good way to end the day.

THE END.

ACKNOWLEDGEMENTS

When I was asked what this story was about, I told people it was a heart story. It was one I knew I needed to write for my children, and their children. It was a tip of my hat to the women that raised me. It was written for all mothers, those beginning their journey and those who are watching their babies grow up and leave home. If you are reading this, then I thank you for your inspiration.

I also want to thank my children, mother, aunts and grandmother - without whom there wouldn't be a story at all. These are the people who taught me what being a family means. The tapestry of my life is better for the threads of yourself that you have woven into it.

I would like to thank those of you who I reached out to, and who gave me their blessing to include our shared memories in this memoir. My support network of amazing friends, both male and female, who always show up and answer the call. A special shout out to Kelly and Sarah, who read through my draft and provided me with feedback and encouragement.

Also, my friend Danielle, who has provided me with endless advice on writing and self-publishing, this story would be gathering dust on a hard drive if it wasn't for you.

I hope you realise how much I appreciate you, that I see you, and my life is richer because of you.

Life truly is awkward and precious.

ABOUT THE AUTHOR

Liss Brewer is a writer, photographer, photographic editor and mother who lives in Brisbane, Australia. She spends her time in the garden, drinking tea and daydreaming.

www.ingramcontent.com/pod-product-compliance
Lightning Source LLC
Chambersburg PA
CBHW070254010526
44107CB00056B/2461